THE AMAZING BOOK OF EVERYTHING

EVERYTHING

Your Complete Guide To Personal Success,
Wealth, Health & Happiness

THE AMAZING BOOK OF EVERYTHING

Your Complete Guide To Personal Success, Wealth, Health & Happiness

EDITED AND COMPILED BY THE
PERSONAL & FINANCE CONFIDENTIAL RESEARCH TEAM

Published by Agora Lifestyles Ltd
Registered Office: 103 New Oxford Street, London WC1A 1QQ
Telephone: 020 7447 4018

Registered in England No: 3303666. VAT No: GB 629 7287 94

ISBN No: 1 899964 92 4

CONTENTS

Why Shouldn't YOU Have More Money, Good Health, The Promotion And Social Life You Deserve

Dear Friend,

Welcome to *The Amazing Book of Everything*. It's crammed full of little-known secrets and tips that your *PFC* team has uncovered for you from around the UK and all over the world.

The net is cast far and wide to ensure that you're brought the most useful, least-known news and information – all condensed down to the bare essentials.

Our researchers are always busy uncovering the hottest news and meeting with the top experts in their field to get you the right information to keep you ahead of everyone else. We receive literally thousands of documents from professional insiders and expert contacts around the world, every year. Each one is thoroughly re-read and verified – so you don't miss out on that one tip that might change your life forever.

Important Secrets Are Being Kept From You

Information the government would like to keep from you... like how to make sure your MP doesn't throw your letters in the bin – we go into this in detail on page 21... And how to have a question tabled for parliament to discuss. The power is already yours – but with *The Amazing Book of Everything*, you now have the tools you need to access it...

Why are financial institutions hiding facts which could radically improve your wealth? If these things were common knowledge, many firms wouldn't make the enormous profits they do now...

Can you imagine your mortgage lender telling you how to save up to £58,000 on a £60,000 mortgage – simply by paying back a little more each month? Of course not – because then they'd miss out on pocketing all that cash themselves! Discover how you can make even greater savings on your mortgage by knowing exactly when to pay...

Most worryingly, your GP may not be telling you all you need to know to protect you health. Let's face it, many GPs are now so overworked and stressed they simply don't have time to read all the latest research. Your doctor may never have heard of the sleep-inducing benefits of passiflora extract. And there's not a surgery in the country which will recommend drinking coffee as a way to minimise cold symptoms, or to limit depression – we examine the evidence on page 69.

This Book Is About Taking Control Of Your Life

And this means developing your mental and social skills too… discover how to develop a super memory and never forget a name or a face again on page 23… or, turn to page 14 to learn how to enter competitions with the winning slogans that bag the prizes… Launch your own money-making enterprise on the internet – turn to page 45… And on page 54, you'll find the secret diet which is based, not on calories or food groups, but on blood types – to help you lose weight and increase your resistance to certain diseases.

With this incredible book you'll know how to get the most out of work, your relationships, the stock market and your own money-spinning business venture. And with the groundbreaking advice *PFC* will continue to uncover and deliver to you every month, you can be confident nobody will be able to take you for a ride again.

Best regards

Helen Elliott (signature)

Helen Elliott
Publisher

P.S. To start making those life-affirming changes, simply turn to page 5 and try *PFC*'s brain workout, five simple exercises that will help you make the most of your potential and improve your work performance – right now!

PERSONAL SUCCESS

USE STRESS TO MAKE YOU MORE SUCCESSFUL

Recent research has found that 40% of us have to take time off work because of stress-related problems. But if you are to perform to your maximum ability, certain levels of pressure and challenge must exist. Balancing your productivity and stress levels is the secret of successful stress management. Here's how to make stress work for you and help you achieve what you want in life:

1. Plan your day. Whatever goals have been set for you by other people, it is important that you have realistic self-goals. It can be helpful to look for various 'small satisfactions' during the course of a job, rather than just a large one at the end. Example: dealing each day with a set number of letters, faxes and phone calls which help towards the completion of a major project should be a source of satisfaction in itself. It is important to accept that yesterday has gone – it can't be repeated nor improved. As for tomorrow, what you do now will shape its course. Concentrate on today.

2. Be true to yourself. The best way of managing stress and turning it to your advantage is to accept the way you are. Acknowledge you're less than perfect – we all are. Look at someone you admire, and identify their weaknesses – everyone has them. Then concentrate instead on what you can do well, and your successes.

3. Identify with others. It's easy to become over-pressured by your interpretation of another person's attitude. Seeing both sides allows you to regain balance. Practise the key skill of listening – with your ears for the words, and your eyes for the body movements supporting them. Accept that everyone will approach life differently. Example: if you consider yourself a perfectionist, others may view you as a 'pain in the neck'.

4. Learn to relax. Discover whatever it is that works for you – whether listening to music, gardening or walking in the countryside. Make sure you budget 'breathing spaces' into your working day so that you can relax regularly – these can be as simple as getting out into the fresh air at tea and lunch breaks. When feeling stressed, simply stop! Train yourself to take deep breaths, look out of the window, or walk around for a few minutes. If you want some peace, put on a pair of personal stereo headphones; even if you're listening to silence, it helps. Then return to what you were doing.

5. Eat and exercise effectively. Eating five small meals a day provides better support for your body than the occasional large one. Drink two litres of water per day to flush through your body's systems. Eat plenty of fresh fruits and vegetables, whole-grain foods (cereals, bread, pasta) and stick to white meat and dairy products for protein. Avoid red meat, salt, sugar, white flour, fats and 'junk' food. Be careful of 'diet' foods – although they may have fewer calories, they are often high in saturated fats. Regular exercise improves the condition of your heart, reduces blood pressure and cholesterol levels, and increases your sense of wellbeing. So, take 20 minutes for a brisk walk three times a week to maintain good health.

6. Learn to fall asleep. Sleep is essential if you're to balance pressures and challenges. Use this breathing process to help you to sleep restfully. Exhale for twice as long as you inhale – count in your head as you breathe in and out. Choose a count you feel comfortable with – but always in a 2:1 proportion. Examples: 6:3 seconds or 8:4 seconds. Keep it all effortless – breathing must be smooth and continuous, without stops or shakiness. Don't pause between exhaling and inhaling, and avoid emptying your lungs. Follow this pattern: eight breaths on your back, 16 breaths on your right side, 32 breaths on your left side. Very few people make it to the end of this routine because it works so well.

7. Use time efficiently. Good time management is one of the essential features of making stress work for you. In particular, make 'to do' lists, and prioritise tasks in order of importance. Allocate realistic deadlines for each task – underestimating the time involved in doing work is a major cause of self-inflicted stress. Do the important tasks at your most active periods of the day, leaving more routine matters to other times. Complete each task before going on to the next one. Don't think about other tasks until you have finished the first one. Avoid juggling paperwork – read it once then act on it, and file it or bin it, as relevant. Once a decision has been made, forget about it and move on. Don't create unnecessary stress by worrying whether it was right or not. Put any uncompleted tasks to the top of your list for the next day.

8. Keep a stress diary. Compile a record of stress-related incidents over the next month. How: divide each day's page into four sections – 'event', 'people involved', 'response', 'ideal response' – and complete as and when you feel stressed. For example, Event: having to deal with too many phone calls. People involved: sales reps. Response: incomplete work, sharp replies, headaches. Ideal response: measured discussions with reps. This diary should enable you to identify problem areas, and devise solutions. For example, turn on answering machine, and return all calls at one convenient time.

FIVE SIMPLE STEPS TO BOOST YOUR BRAIN POWER

You can improve your work performance with a 'brain train' workout – a daily programme of mental skillbuilders that enables managers and their teams to concentrate better, make faster decisions, solve problems more quickly and be more creative. Here's what to do:

1. Thought master. This exercise allows you to build your powers of concentration whilst making you aware of distracting thoughts. Concentrate on the second hand of your watch for one minute, silently repeating the number 'one' as you do this. If a distracting thought comes into your head, maintain your concentration but move to 'two'. If another distracting thought occurs to you, keep concentrating but go on to 'three'. Record your score of intruding thoughts. With daily practice, you will reduce the number of intrusive thoughts – and improve your self-discipline enabling you to concentrate even when you really don't want to!

2. Brain buddies. Your brain comprises a left and right cortex. Think of these as two buddies working together to better your performance. Make time every day to write out two sentences with your non-dominant hand – the one you don't normally write with. Note the time it takes to do this. The next day, do the same again – and every day after that. This workout strengthens the buddy who's been lacking exercise and makes both cortices work more productively.

3. Working tools vocabulary. Words are the working tools of your brain – you need a strong vocabulary to develop your mind. A good strategy is to find a new word to add to your vocabulary each day. Write the word and its definition in your diary and start using it straightaway. You will improve your communication abilities.

4. Whole brain pictures. Think of a different word every day – and create a 'whole brain picture' from it. For example: 'ocean' is an evocative word. In your mind, see yourself walking on a beach and hear those crashing waves. Smell the ocean breeze as you taste the salty spray hitting your face. Touch the sand between your toes. Using this technique you will develop your five senses.

5. Breathing space brain (BSB). Your brain needs to rest occasionally – to relax effectively, you need to develop your 'breathing space brain'. Find some quiet time and space and sit or lie on your back, relax your body and close your eyes. Begin breathing easily, and listen to its sound. If your attention drifts from your breath, bring it back. Continue for several minutes. Repeat the exercise but concentrate instead on a favourite word, such as 'calm', 'peace', 'wealth'. Say the word silently to yourself each time you exhale. Do this for several minutes. You can use BSB whenever you feel stressed out or want to boost your performance. And of course, a good night's sleep also works wonders for boosting your brain power.

HOW TO MAKE YOURSELF LOOK GREAT IN PASSPORT PHOTOGRAPHS

PFC tip: get a good passport photo from a booth by lowering the seat so that the camera is just above the level of your nose – this reduces eye shadows and strengthens your jawline. Next: raise your head – this makes your nose look smaller. Finally: smile – this transforms your face, and makes you look terrific.

SEND YOUR CONFIDENCE SKY-HIGH WITH OUR EASY-TO-FOLLOW TIPS

We all experience moments when our self-confidence falters; perhaps as a relationship ends, or during a period of unemployment. But we can learn from these times, and come back stronger and better than ever. Here's how to stop yourself from having negative thoughts and develop a positive outlook on life:

1. **Start by doing things you're good at.** Having a friendly conversation with a neighbour, playing a computer game, tidying up the household accounts. Focus on the things you can do well, and congratulate yourself along the way. For example, 'I really cheered up George with that chat', 'I've zapped another alien – that's brilliant!', 'I've balanced those accounts quickly – and we've some money left over for a treat'.

2. **Try plenty of new things** – be different, do something you've never done before. Seek out new experiences – surf the internet, take up rollerskating or play bowls, sign up for an adult education course. It is important to view the results as a learning experience, not as a 'win or lose' situation. Encourage yourself to take risks – people with high self-esteem take lots of risks – and accept they'll make mistakes. And, they treat these as part of their learning curve. So, the more mistakes you make, the better – they're a sign of growth.

3. **Congratulate yourself** when you make mistakes. Mistakes show that you're getting better. Make sure you have a list of treats ready, anything from buying flowers or having a bubble bath to going on a day trip. You're telling yourself you're worth it – the more you believe this, the better you'll treat yourself, the more confident you'll feel and the more you'll do.

4. Use 'affirmations'. These are positive statements you say to yourself. For example: "I am Anna and I am loving, capable and joyous!" Affirmations should be pertinent to you and your present situation, be in the present tense, and include qualities you want to develop. These will work into your subconscious mind and produce great results – a loving, capable and joyous person.

5. Watch what you say to yourself. We all talk to ourselves, whether consciously or subconsciously. But there is a danger in talking negatively – it can damage your self-confidence. For example, "Damn it, I'm so disorganised." As a guideline, decide whether you would talk to a friend like this. Instead, say under your breath "Cancel"; and replace it with a gentler alternative such as "I'm usually well organised but occasionally I slip up".

6. Act 'as if'. Until we've regained the confidence we'd like to have, we should act 'as if' we have it. Visualise how a confident person would look. What would they be doing? And what would they be saying? In the process of acting 'as if', you'll discover you have become that confident person. And, find your self-image – this is the image you have of who you think you 'should' be. Make sure this is realistic, and you will achieve it.

MAKE A VIDEO – AND CAPTURE THOSE HAPPY MEMORIES FOREVER

If you want to remember children's birthdays, weddings and other family occasions more easily, video them. And if you want a video that everyone will enjoy watching again and again, follow these tricks of the trade:

1. Plan a story – this makes it easier to film, and more enjoyable to watch. Example: Dad wants to video the family holiday. But: most people get no further than filming the odd swim or day out. Result: a video of limited interest. Fact: most audiences like a story. Better: Dad gets the children to explain where they want to go and why, and what they're doing. Outcome: personalities and places are portrayed, and a story develops. Wise: draft a loose storyline with a beginning, middle and end, and what you want to see within each of them.

2. Pay attention to the lighting – so that the right mood is created on video. Do: try filming in different lighting situations beforehand, to see what works and what doesn't. And: lock the exposure for the duration of a shoot, rather than using the automatic exposure feature. Why: this controls how much light is let in, and can change whilst filming and ruin the shoot. Example: if a white van went through your shot. Also: make certain the overall colour balance is correct. How: if your camcorder has a white balance switch, point the camcorder at a piece of white card that fills most of the frame. And: position the card so that the light is falling on it. Next: check your colour monitor – looking in particular at flesh tones – and redo the white balance until you're happy with it.

3. Think about the sound – off-screen noise and sounds can distract from your story. Unfortunate: a camcorder microphone records all the sound presented to it; including sounds you don't want to hear. Outside: putting a baby's mitten over the microphone can minimise noise on a windy day: Indoors: filming the source of any noise can help to reduce viewers' irritation later; when they would otherwise hear but not see where it was coming from. Note: background chatter often sounds better than an embarrassed silence – and it also helps to relax anyone who is being filmed.

4. Put participants at their ease – so that the video seems natural and real; rather than staged and acted. Important: getting a good 'performance' from your stars means making sure they don't become self conscious, perform or act up. General: keep your filming as unobtrusive as possible. Useful: try to film them doing something they normally do, so they don't have to think about it. Example: you want to film a child opening a present. So: give them the present and let them get on with unwrapping it – don't tell them where to sit and how to open it.

5. Vary your shots – to add variety and interest to the story.

Tip: high angle shots – from the top of a ladder or a roof – can create a feeling of detachment or space. And: moving sideways to follow a person can add a sense of depth to a scene. Also: low angle shots – from a small tripod known as 'baby legs' – can convey a child's eye view. Plus: moving the focus from one person to another or zooming in or out can liven up a lengthy shot. But: resist the temptation to do this more than once or twice. Too often, and it becomes a distraction. Guideline: practise in advance. See what interests you – and when these tricks begin to irritate.

Work with both eyes open – to make sure the story unfolds successfully. Explanation: a camcorder's viewfinder usually comprises a small monitor with an adjustable viewing lens. And: most first-timers keep one on that, and the other one closed. Wiser: train that other eye to stay open to observe the 'real' scene; what's happening nearby, who's coming into shot, etc. And: this can enable you to shoot some unexpected, magical scenes. Examples: a baby's smile, a child's funny walk, a dog chasing its tail.

IMPROVE YOUR CONVERSATION SKILLS

Many people are apprehensive about making conversation with groups and individuals they don't know well. Follow these tips to learn how to speak effectively in public without embarrassment:

1. **Relax consciously by breathing slowly,** and then simply concentrate on keeping eye contact with whoever is speaking at the moment. This shows your interest and willingness to participate, which pleases the other person who will feel involved with you, as they know that they have your attention.

2. **When you feel comfortable,** aim to join in a group conversation without becoming the centre of attention straightaway. Do this by making a warm and sympathetic comment, without disagreeing with the speaker. Or ask a general question. People will feel you are part of the group and this will help you to relax.

3. Be willing to admit at some point that you do not know much about a particular topic and ask for more information. This involves you in more contact with the speaker.

4. Make a more positive contribution to the conversation. Decide to offer a warm compliment: "I think you handled that situation well." A positive contribution helps everyone present to relax and open up.

5. You're now ready to make a contribution of your own – either one idea, or a short example of how something similar happened to you. Keep it brief at this stage, and uncontroversial. A clearly expressed and relevant idea will always be welcomed. Maintain eye contact as you say it. But don't make any attempt to take the idea any further at this stage. Just enjoy the feeling of success.

6. As you begin to enjoy conversations again, your goal should be to introduce a new angle on the same topic; or a related one if the conversation seems to be flagging. Perhaps you can ask someone what they think about a related issue that was raised in this morning's press. You can have planned this topic in advance, and the conversation will then continue on this new topic without necessarily having to involve you again – which leaves you free to relax and enjoy it. Take every opportunity to be with people, rather than cutting yourself off. Also: think about what you intend to achieve each time before entering a conversation, rather than rushing in.

A COMPREHENSIVE GUIDE TO FINDING A JOB ABROAD

Working overseas has never been easier. Why: 14 countries in Europe offer free access to job hunters from the United Kingdom. And: there are many opportunities in other countries around the world. Here's a step-by-step guide:

1. Choose the right country for you. Think carefully about your choice of country; and find out as much as you can about as many as possible before making your decision. Caution: there's a huge difference between holidaying in a country in the summer and working there in the winter. Good: those countries and regions which are less popular with expatriates offer excellent career potential because they are short of experienced, qualified people. Examples: Eastern Europe, Far East.

2. Consider the lifestyle. Only one-third of your day is spent at work – so take account of the accompanying lifestyle. Some countries offer excellent job prospects but a poor quality of life. Examples: Middle East countries. Others provide modest employment opportunities but an excellent, unhurried lifestyle with fine weather. Examples: Spain, Portugal. Remember your family too – your partner's job prospects and your children's education. Essential: try to make at least one non-holiday trip to a country before accepting any job offer.

3. Examine permit requirements. Your chances of getting a work permit and a visa depend on where you are going, who you are and where you're coming from. Fact: sometimes these are granted readily; on other occasions they are almost impossible to obtain. Note: some countries such as America grant them only if the employer can prove local people are not available to do the job. But: European Union citizens don't need a work permit or a visa to work in EU countries.

4. Select the right type of job. It's easy to regard working overseas as a completely fresh start, but this is not a good idea. Reason: most of the opportunities available are for people with significant, relevant experience to offer. This is especially true for well paid jobs. Tip: find a better post more easily by applying for the same job you're doing now.

5. Contemplate a job transfer. Working abroad needn't mean resigning your current position and starting again. Wise: look at transferring overseas within your organisation, to other branches or subsidiaries. Alternative: consider getting a job with your company's foreign suppliers or customers. Always: use your network of contacts to find work. The vast majority of all vacancies are filled in this way in both the United Kingdom and overseas.

6. Exploit your qualifications. Do: find out if they are accepted in the appropriate country and check the procedure to have them recognised there. How: for professional qualifications, consult the issuing body. Also: the Europe-wide network of National Academic Recognition Information Centres can provide advice on the acceptability of academic qualifications in the European Union. Contact: UK NARIC, 01242 260010.

7. Refine your language skills. These are the most important attributes required to find a job abroad. Even in those countries where English is spoken in the business world, you'll get a job far more easily if you can speak the local language. And: you'll need this skill for day-to-day living as well. Tip: invest in a language course before emigrating – it's money well spent.

8. Use appropriate newspapers and periodicals. Spend time in a library to discover which UK and foreign publications contain vacancies relating to the work you want to do. *PFC* recommendation: *The European Newspaper Publishers' Association* has links to all major European newspapers – many in English. Visit their website at **www.enpa.be/e/i-newsp.html**.

9. Use employment agencies. Many employment and recruitment agencies handle overseas vacancies. See the *FRES Yearbook*, published by the Federation of Recruitment and Employment Services. This should be available in larger libraries. Also: the European Employment Services (EURES) network exists so that vacancies which have been notified to the state employment service in one EU country can be accessed through the state employment services in all of the others. Contact your local Job Centre.

10. Apply direct to relevant organisations. Why: this is done by 60% of successful expatriate job seekers. How: write, fax or e-mail prospective employers abroad asking about posts, and outlining your suitability. Do: send a CV with a covering letter to the (correctly named) individual responsible for recruiting in that firm. Best: write in the local language – but only if your command of it is good enough to impress. Useful: build a network of contacts from your own personal knowledge, international *Yellow Pages* and trade directories published by Chambers of Commerce. Try the internet too.

SLOGANS THAT WIN PRIZES

Most people don't enter competitions because they're not sure what to write in the part which says: 'Complete the following sentence in no more than X words.' This tiebreaker section is all-important – it's the 'win or lose' part of most contests, and inevitably determines the winner. But, consistent winning is all about technique – once you've learned the various styles which win prizes, it's simply a matter of deciding which you are most comfortable with and practising. Choose from the following styles:

Play on words: this is a useful technique for a humorous tiebreaker. One winner said that a bicycle shop offered 'wheelie great deals'. The more of a 'groaner' it is, the better. They are always very popular with competition judges. You might win a trip to the Louvre with a line like 'With more taste for less Monet, what have I got Toulouse?'.

Homonyms: use words that sound or are spelled alike, but which have two or more different meanings. For example, a bride won a dream wedding by completing the sentence 'After the wedding...' with 'Aisle Alter Hymn!'

Adaptations: this involves adjusting the titles of well-known films, songs or books to fit the slogan requirements. As an example, 'A Dish called Wonder' won a prize from a manufacturer of cook-in sauces soon after the film *A Fish called Wanda* was released.

Alliteration: put together several words which all start with the same sound. For example, 'It's better with a bit of butter!' It's not necessary to make every word start with the same sound – in some cases it can make it sound too contrived: 'Clever colour creates cosy attention', for instance. But used carefully, alliteration always attracts attention.

Contrasts: use two words of opposite meaning to produce an eye-catching effect: 'High quality goods at a low price' and 'You get friendly hellos and lots of good buys'. Most thesauruses list antonyms – words that mean the opposite – so browse through their pages for inspiration.

Spoonerisms: this technique involves transposing the initial letters of words to create something humorous. As an example, 'mint of history' instead of 'hint of mystery'.

Malapropisms: the 'unintentional' misuse of a word by confusing it with one of similar sound can often produce amusing results. The most mundane of slogans can take on a new look with a malapropism. For example, the slogan for household paint declares: 'They're a pigment of my imagination'. Don't forget to jot down any ones you may hear on a day-to-day basis, as they could come in handy one day.

Rhyming couplets: when in doubt, send in a two-line rhyme. Armed with a good rhyming dictionary, this technique is easy to learn. The trick is to get the rhyme and scansion – the metrical rhythm of the verse – exactly right. Read it aloud, counting the number of syllables in the first line. The number of syllables in the second line must match exactly without being forced. Be careful that your regional accent – whatever it may be – doesn't influence your choice of rhyming words.

Triple rhymes: you can make your rhymes stand out even more by using three rhyming words rather than just two: 'For beauty care and shining hair, Boots is the store that's always there'. Look for more unusual rhymes, rather than the overworked 'test/best', 'savour/flavour', 'treasure/pleasure/leisure' and 'delights/excites/invites' combinations.

Alternatives: other tiebreaker tasks fall into two categories. 1: writing an ending for a limerick involves being given the first line or two and having to make up the rest yourself. To complete it successfully, remember there should be a rhyming 'punchline' in the last line, so it often pays to begin here. Make a long list of words that rhyme – as your punchline must end with one of these, you're getting the most difficult part over with. It's then fairly easy to work backwards, filling in the central couplet. 2: naming a logo character. What you're looking for here is something that's particularly apt to the product. For example, what would be a suitable name for a character who is a regular saver with a bank which pays terrific interest rates? Ivor Lottabrass, perhaps. Flicking through a joke book will give you lots of ideas; the cornier, the better!

PFC tips: study the instructions for clues. Typically, you will be asked to provide an 'apt', 'original' and/or 'amusing' slogan. 'Apt' means appropriate to the goods being promoted, the prize on offer, or the theme of the competition. A good tiebreaker mixes together two or more of these three factors. 'Original': your first thoughts are likely to be similar to those of countless other entrants. Discard them. If two or more entries are similar, they are considered unoriginal, and are scrapped. 'Amusing': there is a thin dividing line between funny and rude. By and large, daring slogans don't win. Picture your judging panel as elderly spinsters and you won't go far wrong. Identify the product's positive features and include these in your slogan. Keep the slogan simple and sincere. Don't go overboard with accolades – they make your entry sound phoney and reduce your chances. Make your slogan unique to the product – if it isn't mentioned in the introductory wording, refer to it by name. Avoid vague statements like 'You've tried the rest, now try the best' which apply to anything. The closer you get to a personalised entry, the better your chances. Don't knock rival products – there's no such thing as bad publicity. As far as you're concerned, they don't exist. Don't ask for a prize. Phrases such as 'I'd like to win a Bermuda holiday because... I've been unemployed for three years and need a break' comprise 25% of entries and never win. Judges are looking for something positive and upbeat.

THE SECRETS OF SUCCESSFUL NETWORKING – BY THE EXECUTIVES WHO'VE MADE IT TO THE TOP

A life-changing career move won't come from the job section of your newspaper. It will come through the people who know and like you, and want you to succeed – friends, family, acquaintances and colleagues. Decide who can help you achieve your goals, and set up a 'network meeting' with the right people. You'll soon make the connections you need to get what you want.

1. **Uncover the potential of your network right now** – list all your friends, colleagues and business associates. Include their postal address, telephone number and e-mail address. Then note how each of them could be useful to you. What or who do they know that they could pass on to you as a useful connection or contact. Don't feel uncomfortable about using your friends or family to help you. Your genuine affection for them means you'll return the favour soon. And they are the difference between scouring the 'Situations Vacant' pages, and setting up a meeting to discuss the new job or contract you want right now.

2. **Maximise the value of your connections** – decide exactly what you want to achieve with their help. You must be clear in your own mind about your goals, or your network won't deliver. To uncover the most lucrative new opportunities, listen to friends for news of new products and services, emerging markets, upcoming retirements, reorganisations, expansions, mergers or take-overs – anything related to change, as change means opportunity. Write down how you want to take advantage of this new situation. If you're looking for a better job, decide on the extra benefits you want. If you want advice on a career change, write down your terms of salary, hours, challenges, training, and status. If you need to expand your own business, estimate how much your next contract should be worth.

3. **Make other people want to help you** – networking is a 'give & get' relationship. The key to successful networking is keeping the conversation as informal and friendly as your relationship already is. And balance the tips,

advice, and new contacts you receive by returning the favour! Look at your list of contacts, and see who could benefit from being put in touch with each other. Then, next time you meet one of your friends or colleagues, mention another friend's skills and suggest how useful they could be. Your friends may suggest other people you should talk to. Make sure you follow through and call this new contact by telephone. Overcome the fear of 'cold calling' by remembering you have a mutual friend. Mention that they suggested you call, and propose an informal meeting.

4. Have the most productive network meetings – remember you're only asking for information and advice. You're not looking to get a job from your first meeting with your new contact. Networking is about developing a mutually beneficial relationship. Asking a new contact about specific jobs at their company could embarrass them. They might advise you to go through the usual personnel department channels – and you will have got nowhere! More importantly, they may feel offended that your mutual friend passed on their details. Instead, have an open discussion with your new contact about your plans, and ask their advice. Do your homework, so you can talk knowledgably about their company. Although it's an informal meeting, dress well. Be optimistic, and make sure you both have fun. Successful job hunters know that networking creates relationships, which in turn create new openings. Focus on the person, not what they might be able to offer you.

5. Let your network bring you new opportunities in the future – stay in touch with your friends, clients, colleagues and business contacts regularly. Call them all at least once a month, to say hello and have a quick chat. You could discover some valuable information. At work, seize every opportunity to participate in seminars, workshops and meetings. Outside work, meet as many new people as you can. Join local clubs, charities and sports teams. Whenever you can, collect business cards from other people, and distribute yours to friends and business associates who can make referrals. Write notes on the back of all business cards you collect, to remind you where and when you met the person and what you remember about them. Update your telephone and mailing list weekly.

Bottom Line: finding a great new opening amongst your friends isn't difficult. Simply look at how they can help you – and how you can help them. Ask your existing contacts to suggest who they think you should meet, and build a relationship with these people. It doesn't really matter who you choose, as long as you like them, they like you – and you have something to offer each other.

MONEY IN A FLASH – HOW YOU CAN SELL YOUR PHOTOS

Your camera can form the basis of a profitable part-time business. All you need is determination and commercial savvy and you'll find plenty of money-making opportunities for good semi-professional photographers. Here are four money-spinners:

1. **Property photography.** Using your local Yellow Pages, telephone all the estate agents in your area. Aim to get a regular order to take photographs of all of the houses the agency is trying to sell. To clinch the deal, offer to photograph the first five houses free of charge. When you arrive, decide how to show the property in the best way. For example: if the house next door has old cars parked in the drive, closed curtains, or rubbish piled by the front door, you'll want to exclude these. Most estate agents want at least one large photograph for their window display and 50 smaller prints for their written particulars. Good photographic shops can supply adhesive-backed 'stickiprints' for easy insertion on to printed particulars. Boost business by suggesting that slow-selling properties should be re-photographed regularly. For example, a photograph of a house in December will be less attractive than one taken in the spring.

2. **School photography.** Contact every school in your area by letter or telephone call. Don't neglect to get in touch with independent schools as well. Aim to photograph every pupil in the school individually. And, offer to take brother/sister photographs, class and year photographs and school teams photographs as well. Negotiate a bulk discount with a photographic shop or a mail order photographic processor. The best size for a portrait photograph is

eight by six inches. Mount photographs inside a neat cardboard frame; and enclose them within a clear PVC case to keep them clean – these items are available from photographic shops. The school is responsible for distributing the photographs to parents and collecting the money. Photographs are offered on a sale or return basis and you will find that the profits from sales more than cover the cost of returns. On average the typical response rate is 65% sales to 35% returns. You would usually expect to have to give 20% of the sale price received as commission to the school. Always contact schools once every year to arrange to photograph the whole school again.

3. News photography. Approach local newspapers, local offices of national newspapers and news agencies to offer your services. Contacts can be found in *The Writer's Handbook* or *Benn's Media Directory* – you'll find copies of these in major libraries. Your chances of being employed will be improved if you have a selection of newsworthy photographs ready to show the news editor. The best photographs will invariably be of people, places and events. If a newspaper agrees to use your services don't wait for them to call you. Make sure you keep your camera with you at all times, take photographs of any newsworthy event (for example, a traffic accident, a demonstration, or an agricultural show) and call the editor immediately with details. As you build up relationships with newspapers, they'll call you out on assignments. Most editors will pay you for any photographs used rather than on an hourly rate basis, but this can be much more profitable for you. Rates vary from £30 for a run-of-the-mill photograph, up to hundreds of pounds for a really newsworthy photograph; perhaps at a demonstration. If you have a photograph of a major incident, you might be able to sell it to national newspapers, and earn several thousand pounds from it.

4. Landscape photography. Take photographs of famous buildings, local scenes and attractive landscapes, and produce a range of framed photo-prints from them. Best bets are widely admired sights that are popular with local people and tourists – for example, beauty spots, cathedrals, churches and stately homes. You probably already have a good supply of photos like this in your holiday albums. Plan the best place and time to take your photographs – buildings and landscapes look better when it is sunny. Take at least ten photographs, then have them developed and choose the best shot. Have five or six copies of this printed and framed. Save money by doing this yourself using ready-made frames purchased from a framing shop. Offer them to local shops on a sale-or-return basis. Home furnishings and craft shops are ideal sales outlets for you. And you can arrange to display your pictures in local pubs and restaurants to sell them to customers. Make sure you check the prices of similar photographs in your area to settle on an appropriate price. On average, a good framed photograph will cost around £3 to produce using ready-made frames, and sell for about £15-20. Offer a commission of 10-15% to shops, pubs and restaurants that sell your photographs.

HOW TO MAKE YOUR MP SIT UP AND BARK LIKE A DOG

If you need help of almost any kind, your local MP can enable you to achieve whatever you want – because they know how the system works, and how to work the system. Get your MP working for you with these little-known tactics:

1. Write to your constituency MP about personal issues – this is the one member of parliament who will really help you. Traditionally, MPs do not take up cases for other MPs' constituents so writing to your local MP is the best way of getting your issue raised – other correspondence receives short shrift. Write to the House of Commons, London SW1A 0AA. Never write direct to a Government Department – you'll receive a non-committal reply drafted by a civil servant. If you write to your MP, you'll get a reply that's at least signed by a minister. It may be the same reply – but you can then contact the MP again to ask if they or the minister read the letter before sending it to you. This is really effective – it attracts the MP's interest who'll pass on your comments to the minister who'll refer it to that civil servant who drafted the reply. This increases the attention given to your problem.

2. Telephone the House (020 7219 3000) for urgent matters and leave a message for your MP to call you back – this way, you'll get a faster response. And when you speak, ask for a personal meeting to discuss the issue. MPs hold regular surgeries in their constituency where they meet constituents.

Unfortunately surgeries are not publicised widely so you'll need to contact your MP or local constituency office. Look in the telephone book under the appropriate political party's name to find out when the next one is being held, and make an appointment. You'll get a more practical response from the MP if you supply some background details before your meeting.

3. Lobby 200 MPs if you represent a pressure group – this is the most effective way to get action. Ten constituency letters sent to one MP on the same subject discloses a serious issue that should be followed up by that MP. And, if 200 MPs each receive ten letters on the subject from their constituents, the Government is alerted to the matter. It is best to encourage constituents to write their letters in their own words. Printed forms distributed by an organisation to its members for signing and forwarding to MPs are usually treated with contempt by MPs. These printed forms suggest that these people have such little interest in the matter that they cannot be bothered to write for themselves.

4. Always ask your MP if they're prepared to table a Parliamentary Question (PQ) about a serious private or public matter – this can have an electrifying effect on resolving your problem. The request will almost certainly be passed to a minister who will ask a bureaucrat to deal with it. And nothing disturbs a civil servant more than having to prepare a PQ for oral answer – it's not only necessary to provide an initial reply, but to counter every conceivable supplementary question as well. This is the reason ministers bring such big books to the despatch box at Question Time; there may be several pages of notes and comments for each PQ that's been tabled.

Bottom line: Civil servants are the same as everyone else; they're not keen on extra work. When they're faced with a constituent who knows how the system operates, they'll usually do all they can to bring matters to the speediest possible conclusion.

REVEALED – 13 MAGIC WORDS THAT WILL SELL ANYTHING

PFC tip: use at least three of the little-known 'power words' in any advertising and sales material, and you'll boost your chances of making a sale. Good words include free, easy, discover, guarantee, new, proven, safety, results, save, you, love, money, health. These words act as the trigger that makes people want to buy goods and services. And the more power words you use, the more likely you are to become a successful seller.

HOW TO ELIMINATE CAR ACCIDENT DISPUTES IN A FLASH

PFC tip: carry a loaded camera or disposable camera in the glove compartment of your car – and take photographs if you're involved in an accident. This minimises disputes about what did and/or didn't happen. Even if the camera isn't loaded, pretend to take photographs – the other driver won't know the camera is empty and is far less likely to lie if they think you've got the photographic evidence needed to disprove their statements.

HOW TO DEVELOP YOUR OWN SUPER MEMORY

Your brain is more powerful than any computer, and can store and recall far more material than you could ever use in your entire lifetime. All you have to do to develop an almost photographic memory is to learn how to retain information in a way that makes it easy to recall. Then you'll be able to remember every number, name, date or fascinating fact you ever heard or read. Here's the inside story on key areas and techniques:

Bulk information. Learning is most effective if you study for periods of 20 to 40 minutes interspersed by regular five-minute breaks. Then spend a couple of minutes thinking over what you have just learned before going on to the next section. Reviewing is important, and should be done at increasingly long intervals. The first review should take place no more than an hour after the learning period. The second review should be carried out a day later and the third review should take place a week later. A full and proper review of any new information fixes it into your long-term memory; and makes it easier to recall at a later time.

Memory training. The four essentials are: 'association', 'visualisation', 'imagination' and 'sensation'. *Association* – stage performers use linking systems which associate the things they need to remember with objects or events. *Visualisation* – if you visualise what you want to remember, you will remember it far more easily than if you just try to file away a word. It also helps if you visualise something that is personal to you, especially if it is something you own or want to own. For example, don't think 'car', think 'Mercedes'. *Imagination* – the more imaginative you are, the easier it will be to remember. Make that Mercedes a vintage model, manufactured in the year your father was born. *Sensation* – as with imagination, the more sensational or bizarre your picture, the easier it will be to remember. So the resultant memory image would be a 1930 Mercedes painted in shocking pink with big green blobs all over it.

Mind maps. These are a simple but effective method of note-taking, which show key thoughts in a round form rather than a straightforward list. Start by putting the subject in the middle of a sheet of paper. Then write the main sub-headings around it in a circle. Draw lines from the centre to each sub-heading before adding more items in circles around the sub-headings. Some people find it helpful to draw bubbles around each item. Next, re-draw your map to re-arrange things in a neater and more logical order – you'll also find that you can make the map more memorable simply by adding little pictures. For example: if your main subject was an apple, draw an apple in the middle of the page and write 'apple' in it. If a sub-heading was apple pie, draw a pie-shape, connect it to the apple with a line and connect your other thoughts ('with blackberries', 'deep-dish', 'cream' and so on) with lines to the pie. To recall the whole mind map, think of the apple, and the other contents will come back to you.

The link system. This links items together by fitting them into a story. For example, you are going shopping to buy bread, bananas, eggs, pepper, paper tissues and face cream. Visualise yourself going into a supermarket. The only bread they have is such a big loaf that you can't see where you're going as you're walking along with it – so you don't spot the banana on the floor. You step on it, and go sliding down the aisle. You swerve to avoid hitting a display of eggs, and collide with a box of pepper that bursts open. This makes you sneeze so much that you grab some paper tissues to wipe your nose, but this makes it so sore that you have to find some face cream to soothe it. The more off-beat your story is, the more memorable it will be. Exaggerate everything and add colours, sounds, and even smells. These help to make the system work. Movement and attachment are important as well, so make things crash into each other, pile them up, slot them together or make them open a mouth and speak the next word.

The Roman room system. Instead of making up a story around items to remember, associate each item with a feature in the room. Use a room in your own home and go round it in the same way. The shopping list could involve the bread propping the door open, a monkey eating bananas on a chair in the hall, and a fried egg pinned to the kitchen door, which you then open to find that it has been booby-trapped with a jar of pepper. You reach for the paper tissues on top of the refrigerator to wipe your nose, and have to use more to wipe up the mess from a pot of face-cream melting on the cooker.

Numbers. All the systems for remembering numbers with more than seven digits work by breaking the number down into separate chunks and then giving a label to each of them. The 'Number-Shape System' uses a set of images that never changes. You can choose your own images to make them meaningful to you, as long as they are the same shape as the number. For instance, 1 is the shape of a pencil, 2 is the shape of a swan, 4 is a sailing boat; and so on. If the number you want to remember is 214, you visualise a swan using a pencil to write on the side of that boat. Variations on this system are the 'Number-Rhyme System' where 1 would be a bun, 2 a shoe, and 4 a door, so you visualise a bun in a shoe by a door; and the 'Meaningful Number System', where 1 is a broom because it has one handle, 2 is a pair shoes, 4 is a table because it has four legs; so you visualise a broom and a pair of shoes on a table.

Names. The main reason why someone forgets another person's name is because they weren't paying attention when they were introduced. They've failed to file the information in a memorable enough way to store it in their long-term memory bank. To remedy this, when you meet someone new, repeat their name back to them. If you can do it without feeling embarrassed, ask how they spell it. Use the name again as soon as you can. Repeat it once more when you say goodbye to that person. That name will be stored permanently in your memory's database.

Your personal items. People lose personal items such as their keys, spectacles or pen because they weren't paying attention when they put them down. Create a special place for the items you misplace regularly. Make it a logical place and visualise it every time you come in to and go out of your home and/or office. Even if you didn't take your keys out with you, check to make sure they are still there.

WEALTH

ARE YOU LOSING £278 EVERY YEAR UNNECESSARILY?

Britain's householders waste around £6.5 billion each year by failing to buy energy-saving appliances and not installing energy-efficient measures around their homes – this works out at £278 per year for every household. The biggest drain on household budgets comes from a lack of roof, loft and cavity wall insulation, draught proofing, heating controls, high-efficiency boilers and energy-saving refrigeration, washing machines and tumble dryers. It is a myth that energy-efficient products are often more expensive than their conventional alternatives. In reality many products – such as cavity wall insulation – cost far less than consumers think and produce big savings, year after year. Most investments in energy-efficiency measures can be recouped in full within three to five years. Added bonuses include 'cashback' offers and grants for people on social security benefits and/or who are over 60 years may also be available to help finance many of these measures. For example, £200 cashback on a condensing boiler, plus grants towards the cost of loft and cavity wall insulation.

PROTECT YOUR PARENTS' LIFE SAVINGS FROM EXORBITANT NURSING HOME FEES

Many older people have had to use their life savings to pay for nursing and residential care; and some have even been forced to sell their homes as well. But such scenarios can be avoided with advance planning. This is what needs to be done:

Problem: more and more elderly people have been going into nursing and/or residential care homes since 1993. Recent legislation shifted the burden of 'care' from the State to local authorities; NHS hospitals then cut down on long-term care beds, and patients occupying these beds were transferred to homes funded by the local authorities. In an NHS hospital, patients are treated free of charge; but when they're moved into a local authority home, that authority is duty-bound to seek to recover the costs of that care from those patients who have assets above certain levels. And this usually means that any savings in excess of £18,500 (and this can include the value of their own home in some instances) can be taken to help pay for care. Local authorities group assets into two categories when assessing how much someone should pay for care. 'Countable assets' include all forms of money, stocks and shares, savings and possibly even a house, flat or whatever. These are all taken into account. Assets such as personal jewellery, furniture, motor cars etc. are disregarded.

Solution: convert 'countable' assets into those other forms of assets that are not taken account of in the assessment process. Also consider giving away assets to those relatives and friends who would inherit them in due course. And use savings to buy some life assurances to 'compensate' your loved ones on your death; and reduce your savings too! Think about sharing ownership of your home with other family members; or even arrange for it to be given away; and then rent it back. Many of these measures will need to be carried out some time before someone goes into care – typically five years – otherwise, the local authority can claim that there was either a 'deliberate deprivation of assets' or 'reckless spending'; and if this can be proved, the assets in question might still be treated as countable assets. It is vital to discuss these ideas with a solicitor who will provide appropriate advice on your personal circumstances.

SEVEN WINNING FRUIT MACHINE SECRETS

1. Play at the right time. Today's fruit machines are controlled by sophisticated programmes which must ensure that the overall payback to punters is maintained at the legal minimum of 70% of takings. Watch a machine before playing it – and move in when previous players have been losing. It's time for a win.

2. Look for newly-installed machines. These machines are often set to give a higher than normal payback for the first week or so; it attracts punters. For a bonus win – a newly-installed machine must also pay out quickly to reach that 70% minimum return.

3. Listen carefully when you insert a coin. If it falls a long way, the coin tubes from which winnings are paid are probably full, and additional coins are being diverted to a lower part of the fruit machine. If the machine is full, it suggests a win is on the way – so keep playing.

4. If you win any type of skill bonus and need some time to work out what to do, press the cancel button. This usually slows things down, and gives you time to make decisions.

5. If you get two holds in succession, have another go. Most machines then offer a third hold – and the symbol that you need for a winning line always seems to fall into place third time around.

6. When you win a nudge but don't have a winning line, nudge two matching fruits on to the win line. If the next play produces a hold, spin all three reels – and the win should come in.

7. If you have a win above the win line and the machine gives you a hold,

always hold all three reels together – they should then all nudge down as one; and give you that winning line, and even the jackpot.

THE SECRETS YOUR MORTGAGE LENDER WON'T TELL YOU

For most people, buying their own home will cost them about three times its value. They will typically pay around £200,000 for a £70,000 house. The interest payments alone will add up to about twice the price of the house. Instead you can pay off your mortgage years ahead of time and save thousands of pounds in interest payments. Redeeming your mortgage early and paying less is easy. All you have to know is how the system works; and how to beat it.

The system: whatever type of mortgage you choose, you'll have to pay interest, and accumulate enough capital to repay the original amount. This interest is the big addition to the cost of your home – and is where you can save the most money by making payments that reduce the capital on which future interest payments are calculated.

Beating the system: simply pay more than you have to each month. This reduces the effects of compound interest on your original loan. Write to your lender, indicating that you wish to increase your payments. Ask for this to be agreed in writing and request a breakdown of how these overpayments will affect your mortgage and what your new redemption date is. Alternatively ask your lender to work out how much extra you will have to pay each month to reduce your mortgage term by a specified number of years. Paying more than you have to acts as an insurance policy – it allows you to miss one or two payments later when your budget may be stretched without incurring penalties.

Example: to illustrate the effects of paying extra each month, consider this scenario based on a repayment mortgage at 10% interest over a 25-year term. Amount borrowed: £60,000. Contractual payment: £501 per month. If you increase your monthly payments to £540, your revised mortgage period would be 20 years, and you'd save £20,700. Pay £612 a month, and the mortgage period would be 15 years, and the savings would be £40,140. If you pay £771 a month, the mortgage period would be 10 years; and you'd save £57,780 – on that £60,000 mortgage.

Caution: be aware of how mortgage lenders make money from borrowers. Some lenders leave overpayments in limbo until their year-end, when the extra amount is set against your mortgage. In effect, you're giving your lender an interest-free loan. As a remedy put the extra payments into a high-earning, savings account where it will earn interest – then transfer it across to your mortgage account just before the lender's year end. Many mortgage and financial advisers suggest it is better to adopt this method and overpay your mortgage once a year; including interest on your savings. Also, overpayments to building societies are normally deducted from the outstanding capital once a year; usually on 31 December. Make sure your annual repayment is made just before the appropriate date, not immediately afterwards which would mean you'd have to wait a whole year before obtaining the benefits. Some lenders charge a penalty for early or extra repayments – check this and ask your lender to provide written details to compare the benefits with the charges levied. Many lenders set minimum thresholds for overpayment; between £250 and £1,000.

Tip: when interest rates drop, don't be tempted to reduce your monthly payments – continue making payments at the higher level. Try to repay as much as you can when interest rates are low to achieve even higher savings. Also, endowment mortgage holders should review their policy and investment performance at regular intervals to be sure that it keeps pace with the amount outstanding on the mortgage. Re-arrange your policy to ensure it matures at the same time as the amended repayment date for your mortgage.

HOW TO ADD 40% TO YOUR ANNUAL BONUS

PFC tip: increase your annual bonus by as much as 40% by using a tax-boosting tactic known as a 'bonus waiver'. For example, an employer proposes to pay a bonus of £10,000 to an employee. Cost to employer, £10,000 bonus plus reduced National Insurance contribution – a gross cost of £10,700.

Received by employee: £10,000 minus £4,000 income tax (assuming the employee's income is subject to higher-rate tax at 40%) – a net receipt of £6,000. Alternatively if the employee waives their right to any bonus, the employer can probably pay this sum into an occupational pension scheme as a lump sum within Inland Revenue limits. The normal 15% restriction on member contributions is overcome because it is an employer contribution, rather than the employee's. And, this tactic will not at present attract an employer's National Insurance contribution on the payment, so the employee's benefits from the gross contribution are paid into their pension fund.

OWN A FABULOUS FRENCH PROPERTY FOR AS LITTLE AS £4,500

In France, a Provencal house means Provencal prices, but the PFC team of researchers has found areas that have all of the charm of that fashionable area of southern France; and at a fraction of the price! Where: west of the Rhone Valley lies the plateau of Massif Central. You can find a tumbledown cottage there for as little as Fr40,000 (£4,500). Restored farmhouses start at only Fr230,000 (£25,600). And for a maison de maitre with stables and outbuildings, expect to pay from as little as Fr650,000 (£72,200).

HOW TO GET JUST ABOUT ANYTHING YOU WANT FREE OF CHARGE

You can obtain lots of freebies if you know where to look, and what to do. Here are some of the easiest and best freebies that you can get in and around the United Kingdom:

Free food: people spend a fortune on food from health food shops – but much of it is produced from freely available wild plants. A little time spent studying a well-illustrated guide book on wild plants will tell you what you can eat and what to avoid, and will enable you to find plenty of tasty snacks to supplement your diet; and all for free. Examples include wild garlic which grows by rivers and streams. The dried leaves of wild blackberries make an excellent tea substitute. If you prefer coffee, it can be made by roasting acorns. Dandelions fried in flour taste like mushrooms. Nettles can be used for spinach. Crab-apples mixed with elderberries make a delicious jam. Roast lamb will taste even more succulent with sauce made from wild mint. Be careful: do not forage for food in the countryside without first getting the permission of the landowner.

Free magazines, newsletters and other publications: if you're thinking of subscribing to or advertising in a publication and want to check it out first, telephone the publisher's subscriptions and/or advertising department, and ask for a sample copy or what's known as a 'media pack'. This is a package that is sent out to prospective advertisers; and usually contains an advertising rate card, readership details, a copy of the current issue, and, more often than not, several back issues as well.

Free entertainment: there are many venues that offer entertainment for visitors without charge. Examples: the Sizewell Nuclear Power Station in Suffolk offers guided tours for visitors (01728 653653). The Houses of Parliament in London may be visited too – your local MP can arrange a guided tour, and get tickets for you to watch Prime Minister's Question Time. Details: write to your MP c/o the Houses of Parliament, Westminster, London SW1A 0AA; or look in your telephone directory under 'Members of Parliament' for the address and telephone number of the local constituency office. The BBC and independent television companies and radio stations often record shows in front of live audiences. Tickets for these shows are free on application, simply by writing to the 'Ticket Unit' at the appropriate television company or radio station. Ask to be put on the mailing lists for details of forthcoming recordings, request tickets well in advance, and enclose a first class, stamped addressed envelope to encourage a prompt response. Be aware that many game shows are recorded in blocks; so you may see three or four shows in the same visit – that'll give your whole family an experience to remember.

Free tourist information: when planning a foreign holiday, write to the tourist and cultural departments of the appropriate country's embassy in the United Kingdom. Most of these are based in central London – call 'directory enquiries' for a contact number. You will be sent maps, guidebooks and other documentation free of charge; and these will contain the type of useful information that is normally only contained in expensive guidebooks.

Free buildings: long-term building projects such as office block developments are often managed and supervised from a group of Portakabin buildings located on the site of the works. These buildings are usually hired for the period, but are sometimes purchased outright by the developers, who will then often donate these buildings to local charities once the project has been completed. Phone the property developer and ask if they plan to dispose of any buildings on completion of the work. If so, the chances are that they'll give you free, long-term use of a building; you'll probably have to pay for its collection, which may involve the hiring of a lorry to transport it to a new location – but this will only be a fraction of what the building would normally cost.

Free land: a common method of acquiring land is by 'annexing' it. For example, you may have some wasteland at the bottom of your garden. If you extended your fence to cover it, you may be entitled to claim it as your own after a 12-year period has elapsed. The almost forgotten Statute of Limitations Act of 1977 forbids any claims to be made against you by the owner of the land after 12 years. However, note that at any time during those 12 years, the owner could reappear with a writ to order you off their land. And you must try and trace the landowner during the period and be able to show a court that you have done so – but if they cannot be found, you can then apply to a court to have the land registered to you. These final stages should be dealt with by a solicitor.

PFC advice: even when you have to pay for goods and services, aim to achieve a better price by haggling. In some countries, haggling over the price of goods is considered perfectly normal. And in others, it is common practice to give customers a free gift if they spend above a certain amount. Nowadays, more British shopkeepers are prepared to haggle to win business – particularly if they are surrounded by lots of competitors. However, do be aware that traders who allow haggling will expect you to honour your part of the bargain and pay up straightaway. So never start haggling until you are ready to purchase the goods there and then. London's Tottenham Court Road is the top place to haggle for electronic and computer goods; get brand new hi-fis, computers and cameras at substantial discounts.

THE SECRET TAX-SAVING STRATEGIES OF THE TOP TAX ACCOUNTANTS

You could pay anything up to £1,000 per hour to obtain the advice of a top tax accountant in the City of London. But we've done it for you; here's the tax-avoidance strategies they recommend to their clients:

Tax free savings: various investments provide a tax-exempt return – with no tax deducted or to pay at a later date. National Savings: savings certificates pay a fixed rate of compound interest over a five-year period – proceeds are tax-free. Index-linked certificates accumulate in line with the retail price index. Hold your certificates for the full five years, and you'll get a bonus. Using the National Savings Bank allows you to receive the first £70 of interest paid tax-free.

'Age allowance trap': although older people benefit from an increased age allowance, this may be reduced if your income exceeds a certain figure, resulting in a lowering of the tax code. If the excess income is from interest or dividends, you can avoid the reduction in personal allowance by transferring your capital to an alternative form of investment – thus retaining your full, enhanced allowance.

'Personal Pension tax havens': subject to certain, age-related limits set by the Inland Revenue, all the money that you contribute to an approved pension scheme of any kind will attract income tax relief at your highest rate. Your money will be free of capital gains tax and you'll be able to take a tax-free lump sum at retirement age. As a tax-efficient investment, this method of providing money for the future has few equals – it is a way of having your own tax haven for your exclusive benefit. But, and it is a big but, low interest rates mean smaller pensions. Today you need twice as big a pension pot to get the same pension as in 1990.

Unclaimed millions: pensioners and other people on low incomes who believe that too much tax has been deducted from any interest received from bank and building society accounts or other interest-bearing securities, should contact their local Inland Revenue office for advice. It is estimated that millions of pounds worth of rebates are waiting to be claimed. But note that you can't reclaim tax on dividends from UK securities even if you are a non-taxpayer.

Capital gains tax (CGT): gains or profit resulting from the sale of most assets are potentially subject to capital gains tax. Planning and timing are important key factors to consider when seeking to reduce your CGT liability. Make sure you use both spouses' annual exemption – this is the amount of gain you can make in a tax year before CGT is payable. Both husband and wife have an annual exemption. Take gains to avoid wasting the annual exemption – unused annual exemptions cannot be carried forward for the future. Make certain that you carry forward capital losses if they are not used to mitigate CGT this year.

Inheritance tax (IHT): this is both a gift tax and a death duty. It is levied on what you give away in your lifetime and what passes to your estate on your death; these are collectively known as chargeable transfers. And: there is a 'nil rate band' available to everyone. This is similar to the personal allowance for income tax; and represents the amount that you can give away tax-free during your lifetime and on your death. The total transfers made within seven years of death in excess of the nil rate band and the amount passed to your estate on death in excess of the nil rate band are subject to inheritance tax.

Reducing the IHT bill: find out the current nil rate band – if your total assets do not exceed this band, you don't have a problem. But, do remember to include the value of your home when adding up your assets. If you do have a potential IHT liability, there are various ways of reducing it – or even eliminating it altogether. One drastic approach is to give away everything you have now and live for a further seven years – the transfer will then be tax-free. But this is impractical and undesirable for most people. It's better to take advantage of the fact that transfers between husband and wife are exempt from IHT; so if you leave everything to your spouse in your will there will be no IHT liability on your death. The IHT problem may recur when your spouse dies. Also, equalise your estates; as both husband and wife have their own nil rate band you could share your assets, and (if you can afford to) write your wills so that on the first death an amount equal to the nil rate band passes to your children and the balance to your partner. When the surviving partner dies the nil rate band applies again. This option places an amount equal to the nil rate band outside the reach of the Inland Revenue. And you and your spouse can each give away an amount up to the 'annual exemption' limit and can also hand over as many small cash gifts to as many people as you like. Children and grandchildren can be given sizeable gifts as and when they marry. Gifts to charities and for national purposes are exempt from IHT, as are gifts to main political parties.

Warning: remember that your estate will be taxed at the prevailing rates at the time of your death; which may not necessarily be the same as the current arrangements. Any plans you make must be flexible enough to allow for future changes. The gift of an asset must be a genuine and outright gift – if you attach conditions to a gift, it may fall outside of current legislation and a tax liability might be created. Artificial gifts – such as selling an asset for far less than it is actually worth could also cause problems with the Inland Revenue.

PFC alternative: instead of preserving your assets for your children, a radical alternative is to spend them in your lifetime; and leave little or nothing on your death. If you are insurable you can take out a suitable life assurance policy which is placed 'in trust' for your children or other beneficiaries and will pay an amount equal to what you would like to leave on your death. The proceeds of such a policy will then be free of inheritance tax; and you will have the benefit of the use of your own money now. The premiums for the policy can be taken from today's income or assets. Tip 1: If you already have life policies, these can be converted easily to 'in trust' status. Tip 2: Marry before you die. That delays IHT and your partner might be entitled to a widow(er) pension from your works pension scheme if it has one.

PROTECT YOURSELF AGAINST INTEREST RATE RISES

PFC tip: you can protect yourself against your bank's interest rate rises by 'capping' them; it's your own personal insurance policy. To do this you must pay a premium to buy a 'Base Rate Cap' contract from your bank. And, at the end of each quarter, you'll be compensated by your bank for the difference between the strike rate and the base rate on your contract – if the rate rises over the strike rate during that period. **Bottom line:** employ this little-known tactic during stormy economic trading times, and freeze your borrowing fees.

MAKE MONEY IMPORTING & EXPORTING AS YOU TRAVEL

If you're looking to set up a business that involves no capital, no risk and offers plenty of profit, become an import agent. It's a great moneymaker – and you can even do it on a part-time basis from home. Here's what you need to know:

1. Understand the role of an import agent – so you can decide if it's what you want to do. Details: an import agent acts as a go-between; introducing foreign sellers and home-based buyers to each other. Note: they don't get involved in buying and selling goods themselves – so there's no capital outlay or financial risks. And: for these introductions, they receive a commission from the seller based on the value of any transactions – anything from 2.5% to 15%. Typical: 10%, and this is based on the gross value before shipping and handling costs are deducted – so the potential to make big money is there for you.

2. Identify the best markets to export from – this way, you'll be able to discover those overseas exporters that are worth dealing with. Tip: look at those countries with a weak currency that makes their exports cheaper, and more attractive to importers. Examples: Eastern Europe, South Africa, the Far East. And: seek small – to medium-sized manufacturers that wish to export, but cannot afford to employ a permanent overseas sales force. Recommendation: establish links in those countries where you also have a personal affinity – family, friends, some knowledge of the culture, language and/or business workings. Why: this gives you the unique selling point (USP) needed to become a successful go-between between exporters and importers who are unfamiliar with each other's ways. Example: if you were raised in Asia and still have relatives there, make the most of these USPs.

3. Pick the right products to import – that way, it will be easier to find home-based buyers for them, and you can make more money for yourself. Advisable: go for tried and tested items – gifts, crafts, novelties and decorative objects such as jewellery and furniture. Don't: become involved in Far Eastern nursery items and toys – UK import regulations are very strict for these items. Note: knives, weapons, combat and self-defence manuals cannot be imported into the UK. Avoid: plants, perishable produce and electrical goods that often run on different voltages/currents, and do not meet UK safety laws. Hint: household goods are always worth consideration – most countries have their own ranges that are not available overseas, but would often be popular there.

4. Start building your contacts – and set up your money-making business. Best: attend international trade fairs – all prospective exporters from a particular country will be there, seeking to make contacts with importers and agents. Remember: agents receive commission from the seller, not the buyer – so concentrate on looking for manufacturers to start with. Useful reading: International Trade Show Directory should supply details of upcoming fairs – call the publishers on 020 8508 8856 for information. Then: approach UK trade associations for lists of their members – and contact these would-be buyers. Alternative: advertise in trade association publications. Recommended reading: the Directory of British Trade Associations should provide you with contact details for more than 650 associations – find the directory in your local, larger library. Essential: make sure you've a written agreement with the seller before introducing buyers to them. This should guarantee that commission will be paid on all sales made to buyers introduced by you. Bottom line: once you've introduced sellers and buyers, you'll then earn commission on initial and repeat deals too – so you can sit back, and watch your business grow and grow.

FIVE KEY QUESTIONS YOU MUST ASK YOUR INDEPENDENT FINANCIAL ADVISER

You can find the right IFA for your needs by asking five key questions:

1. Who regulates you? Make sure they are registered with a regulatory body such as the Financial Services Authority (0845 606 1234). This means you will also be covered by compensation schemes run by the regulatory body – although there is no protection against investments that just do badly. That's why you should ask these additional questions:

2. What are your qualifications? Check their business card for one or more of these abbreviations. CeFA, CIP, IAC, MLIA (Dip), ITC. It's important to see if they have also passed relevant Financial Planning Certificate examinations in those areas that they're advising you about. Obtaining advanced qualifications shows an advanced understanding of more complex financial issues, such as inheritance taxation. Look for these abbreviations: AFPC, PIC, AIFP, ALIA (Dip), FLIA (Dip), MSI (Dip), AMSI (Dip), MSFA, ACII. Top qualifications: FCII, FSFA, FIFP, FIA, FFA.

3. What are your personal areas of expertise and experience? Few IFAs can offer quality advice on all aspects of personal finance; the majority of them specialise in one or more areas. Be wary of any IFA who promises advice on all conceivable topics. You'd be better off looking for a firm that contains a mix of advisers who cover topics of relevance to you. Newly qualified advisers may be keen, but are unlikely to be as good as someone with several years of experience behind them. Pick an experienced IFA, and one with clients who are similar to you.

4. How do you receive your income? It is sensible to negotiate a fee for advice in advance – commission-only payments tend to be higher; and they encourage some IFAs to recommend products that generate the most commission for them. Typically (high-commission paying) endowment mortgages are suggested instead of (low fee-paying) repayment mortgages. If you decide to buy a product that includes a commission payment to the IFA, ask for a proportion to be paid back to you. Ideally this sum should be the difference between what you would have paid as a straight fee and the total commission involved in the transaction.

5. What ongoing services do you provide for clients? Essentially your financial adviser should be chosen on a long-term basis. Avoid someone who is just starting out – they may move on shortly. And don't pick someone who is approaching retirement. Pick an IFA of similar age and circumstances to you – they'll have a better knowledge and understanding of your situation, may share the same sort of views and opinions, and can work with you as your circumstances change through to retirement.

HOW TO BOOST YOUR CREDIT STATUS

Anyone can improve their credit status – all they need to do is know how lenders think, and learn the tricks of the trade. This is the inside story:

1. Recognise how the system works – so you can work the system to your advantage. When you apply for credit, the prospective lender will base their decision on their credit scoring system and information contained in a credit reference agency's files. Credit points are allocated according to answers given on your credit application form. For example: five points if you rent your home; ten points if you own it. A home owner is considered more creditworthy than a tenant. If your overall score reaches the lender's pass mark, your application will be approved; lower, and it will be rejected. Credit reference agencies keep files on millions of addresses. These contain information on who has lived there, county court judgements, bankruptcy orders, credit searches and other credit details. A would-be lender will refer to your file and reject your application if it contains adverse information.

2. Have a positive reason for applying for credit – and you're far more likely to obtain it. Lenders look more favourably on what they consider to be 'good' (car, home, household improvements, private schooling, weddings) rather than 'bad' (new business start-ups, debt consolidation, political aspirations) applications. Minimise the chances of rejection by avoiding shopping around to various lenders. Multiple applications show up on credit reference agencies' files – and will be viewed with suspicion. It looks as though you are desperate for funds. Boost your chances of sucess – apply to one lender, and preferably one who knows you well.

3. Follow up credit rejections – and discover why you've been turned down. A lender is legally obliged to give you a general reason for rejection. But often rejection letters are bland and non-committal. Identify the real reason by telephoning the company. They won't give you the precise reason, but most will give the broadest possible hint. If it is a credit-score rejection, consider re-applying elsewhere, as all lenders score differently, and another lender may accept an identical application from you. Also, you are entitled to know if the lender has consulted a credit reference agency, and which one. If it is a credit-reference rejection, you will need to check your files.

4. Request your files from the two main credit reference agencies – so you can identify any possible errors. Contact: Equifax, PO Box 3001, Glasgow, G81 2DT. (0845 600 1772). And: Experian, PO Box 8000, Nottingham, NG1 5GX. (0870 241 6212). These files can be unreliable so always apply to both agencies. You will discover they each hold different (and incomplete) information about you. Provide your full name and address, with any other addresses you've lived at during the past six years, plus a cheque for £2 to each agency and your files will be sent to you within seven days. If these include mistakes, the relevant agency must amend them. If you aren't satisfied with any amendment, you can send a notice of correction of up to 200 words. This must be added and sent out to prospective lenders whenever future searches are made.

5. Take some easy-to-follow steps – and improve your overall credit rating. Apply for a credit card – lenders look more favourably on card-holders as they're assumed to be more responsible with credit. Boost your rating further – pay more than the minimum repayment each month. Try to have any adverse information removed from your files – by asking the lenders who registered the information to remove it. Some will agree, if you have subsequently brought payments up to date.

PFC tip: don't send for mail order catalogues too often. Some catalogue companies conduct credit searches before an order has been placed even though credit terms may never be requested. This can damage your credit status. Similarly be wary of paying for car and home insurance policies by instalments – again, credit searches may be recorded on your file. Check your credit reference agency files every six months, and add notices of correction, where appropriate.

YOUR OWN PC FOR JUST £15 – AND OTHER UNBELIEVABLE BARGAINS

If you know where to look and what to do, you can pick up a whole host of unbelievable bargains – an exercise bicycle for £2, a fax machine for £5, a television for £10; even a home computer for only £15. Here's how:

Where: auction sales specialising in repossessed goods and where most of the vendors are organisations such as the Inland Revenue, Customs & Excise and/or finance companies – those that have repossessed items from the original owners or seized them to meet unsettled debts. Private individuals who are selling goods at auction want to obtain the best price and will often set a high 'reserve' price – below which the goods will not be sold. But organisations that are selling by auction are more interested in a speedy, trouble-free disposal of the goods than in getting the best possible price for them. They may wish to sell the goods at any price – and might even be obliged by law to do so. They'll seldom place a reserve price on anything. And if there isn't a reserve price, then the highest bid – however low that may be – is successful. Bottom line: if an easy sale produces a low – or even a ridiculous price – so be it. Most auctions are attended mainly by dealers who intend to resell what they buy at a profit later on – so everything will go at rock-bottom prices – you'll be paying far less than the retail or even wholesale prices.

How: to identify the right type of auction, look at the auctioneer's catalogue. Check the lots for phrases such as 'The Inland Revenue', 'On behalf of HM Customs & Excise', 'By order of the County Court Bailiffs' and 'By order of the Liquidators'. When you see these types of organisation listed, you can be pretty certain there won't be any reserves on these lots, or that they'll be very low. You can also telephone HM Customs & Excise, finance companies, bailiffs, liquidators, local authorities, and repossession firms in your area – and ask them which auctioneers they use. Call the Department of Trade and Industry's 'Insolvency Service' on 0121 698 4000 and ask them for the contact details of the Official Receiver to discover which auctioneers are used.

What to do: view lots carefully before bidding – a bid is almost always legally binding. If there are several similar lots, don't try to get the first one – you'll find the later ones go for lower prices. Decide on the top price you're prepared to pay, and stick to this – it's very easy to get carried away in the excitement of the bidding, and to bid more than you intended to do. In addition to your bid price, you'll have to pay a buyer's premium of around 10% and VAT on the bid price and that premium. Attend at least two auctions as a spectator to get a feel for how it all works.

CLAIM YOUR PLACE IN THE SUN
NEXT YEAR – FREE

Air Miles are firmly entrenched as a free incentive on many products and services. More glamorous than pension plans and free from taxation they've been fought over in the divorce courts and bequeathed in wills! In short, they are ideal perks with which to reward yourself and they will save you money.

You don't need to be a frequent flyer to benefit – around six million people in Britain now collect their Air Miles through an entirely different scheme. To qualify for frequent flyer miles you have to buy tickets from one airline or group of airlines. But over 200 companies are working with Air Miles, the British Airways subsidiary that leads the scheme, to provide their customers with extra incentives to shop with them. To open an air mile account use their website at www.airmiles.co.uk or phone 0870 551 7711. Many retailers also have their own schemes and you can merge existing accounts to reap maximum benefits.

Collecting air miles in your high street. If you shop at Tesco's and you don't yet have a reward card – get one. Then use your points to collect air miles rather than reducing your shopping bill. Look out for special offers and double-point promotions – they can increase your miles-money ratio! Shell's smart points (1 point for every 1 litre of petrol) can be converted to air miles (1500 points gets you 100 miles) but you must register your preference for air miles when you apply for their smart card. Website blissonline.com offers one mile for every £5 spent. In fact websites are often very generous as they are still trying to find an established market and are willing to pay for customer loyalty. And some high street names will give you extra air miles if you order from them online – Laithwaites.co.uk give you 50 miles per 12 bottles bought.

Collecting air miles at home, on holiday or even at work. Paying bills is never much fun – but a number of utility suppliers now offer air miles as an incentive – a cheering prospect. BT Cellnet give one mile for every £5 you spend on calls and line rental, plus an additional 175 miles for joining the network. And you can claim up to one mile for every £2 on your gas bill. Other bonuses come from the RAC (up to 300 miles on becoming a member), Scottish Hydro Electric (900 miles), and Petplan (120).

Air miles can be earned on flight, ferry and holiday bookings too – these are some of the best offers. If you book flights or package holidays through the Air Miles holiday hotline (0870 5577733) you earn a mile for every £5 spent – it soon adds up – and you can choose to save these miles or trade them in for an immediate discount. If you book an Irish Ferries holiday or a return Irish Ferries crossing you can earn up to 1 mile for every £4 spent and P&O Portsmouth offer 1 mile for every £5 spent on tickets over £30.

Some companies offer their employees air miles as incentives to boost sales or rewards for success. If your employer doesn't have such a scheme in place – suggest it today!

How to use your miles to get great deals. Use the Air Miles website, call 0870 5577788 or go through one of the major companies mentioned above to redeem your miles. You can buy leisure or luxury items, and of course, travel. The UK Air Miles company says that at least two people take off with them every minute of the day. Be warned, however, the Air Miles company does not recommend last minute booking – the most popular routes are often booked up well in advance. Do check the *Mail on Sunday* – they promote special competitive offers every week.

Substantial savings can also be claimed on cruises, ferries, trains, hotels, car rental and excursions. Savings on international train fares can be up to 45% and include the Venice to London Orient Express, the Eastern Orient Express and the British Pullman. For 200 miles plus £40 cash you can take the Eurostar to Brussels, Paris or Lille. Savings are also available on days out such as Alton Towers, the London Eye and Kew Gardens.

Bottom Line: With a little careful shopping around and without breaking the bank, air miles can make your money go further. Who knows, this time next year could see you on the holiday of your dreams.

EARN MONEY ON THE INTERNET

Business and the internet are made for each other because businesses have products and/or services to sell and are constantly looking out for new ways to reach their target audiences. The internet boasts a population of millions. Here's how to make money on the net:

1. Decide what you're going to sell via the internet. The value of internet advertising depends largely on what you are selling. For example: if you're publicising a book that condemns the harmful effects of technology, internet users are unlikely to respond favourably. But if you are selling 'I Love Cyberspace' t-shirts, you might just have a seller on your hands. Businesses that trade information are ideally suited to the internet. Information is the most valued commodity on earth – more money is made in media and information-related businesses than in anything else. A business that trades information has most to gain from cyberspace.

Evidence: for years, people have used mail order as a way of selling valuable information. The late Joe Karbo made a multi-million-dollar fortune by self-publishing a 150-page book entitled *The Lazy Man's Way To Riches*, which he advertised extensively in newspapers and magazines. Personal example: perhaps you know how to cook traditional Californian cuisine; you could have 101 of your best and unique recipes printed in booklet form and sell these through small advertisements in the press. Alternatively imagine running your own mail-order company which sells valuable information – but without having to spend money on printing and mailing it to your customers. If a business could sell information whilst dispensing with paper and ink, its overheads would be slashed to the bare minimum, and the profit potential increased to the maximum. The internet offers just this opportunity.

2. Advertise on the bulletin boards of newsgroups to reach your target audience. An internet customer can then e-mail their order to you, together with credit card authorisation details; you simply send the purchased information over the internet for downloading to a PC and printing out as hard copy, as required. And a lucrative business transaction that would have taken days in the world of conventional mail order has taken just minutes on the internet. Less money is spent on paper, ink and mailing which means bigger profits. And less time is consumed by the preparation and despatch of your product; leaving you with more hours per week to enjoy your new-found wealth. Also, your customer is more than happy at being able to order an information product and receive it directly over the internet, rather than having to wait days for a reply by mail.

PFC advice: you now need to come up with an information product that has the commercial potential to be a huge earner. Many celebrities use the internet regularly. Consider sourcing and selling a directory of celebrity e-mail addresses to other cyberspace users who can then send their fan-mail direct. If you have the Midas touch when it comes to gambling or competitions, try selling the secrets of your success to other internet users in online winners' guides. Or maybe you're a whizz at scrabble, playing the guitar or salesmanship – anything which you can do better than the average person could be the basis of a profitable business. Write your own 'How to' guides and sell them on the web.

Bottom line: the number of ways that you can make money on the internet is limitless – confined only by your own imagination. And don't think that you need to charge high prices to make big money – if you can sell an information product for just £1 to only 0.1% of internet users, you'll create a gross profit of £30,000; and you could be earning that within a two-to three-week period!

REMEMBER TUPPERWARE PARTIES? HERE'S A CLUB THAT COULD REALLY MAKE YOU RICH!

Investment clubs offer a relatively low-risk, low-cost route to buying and selling shares. They're fun, exciting and very sociable. Pooling your cash through a club gives everyone more money to play with. And by discussing your investment strategy regularly, you can make better-informed decisions. In the last four years, the number of investment clubs in the UK has grown from 300 to over 8,000. Last year's most successful club, the Golden Eagle Nest Investment Club from Yorkshire, made gains of over 2,439% in just twelve months! Here's how you and your friends can start playing the markets for profit too:

1. Running an investment club is simple – gather together a group of your friends, pool a small amount of money each month, and use it to buy shares. As shares give higher average returns than most investments, it makes sense to invest in the stock market. Few are confident enough to take the plunge alone though. Investment clubs make it easy for you to share the risk, and learn from the expertise of other people – all while having lots of fun. But experienced investors can gain a great deal from being involved in a club too. Clubs work as a DIY unit trust, with the members making the investment decisions rather than a professional fund manager. The more people you have researching and sharing information, the better investment decision you'll make.

2. Share profitable investments with your closest friends – invite three or four to join you for an exploratory meeting. Talk about the principles behind your investment club, and identify other like-minded friends who might be interested. There can be up to 20 members in a club, and with everyone making a monthly contribution the value of the share portfolio soon adds up. Now hold an informal meeting (down the pub is perfect!) to discuss what is involved in setting up and running the club. Discuss and decide how much everyone is willing to invest every month – between £25 and £50 per person per month on average. Find out how often your fellow members would like to meet – once a month is usual. Now pick a regular venue for your meetings. Finally, write out a club constitution and proposed rules for membership. You can obtain draft copies of these important documents in ProShare's Investment Club manual. Send the proposed constitution and rules to all potential members, and invite them to your first formal meeting.

3. Make running your club simple and safe – have potential members choose a chairman, a secretary and a treasurer. All these positions are honorary, but are vital if your club is going to profit and have fun. The chairman encourages everyone to play an active part in all meetings. The treasurer accounts for everyone's cash investments, and the secretary arranges the paperwork. Your first proper meeting must also decide which stockbroker and bank you're going to use. All new members then sign the Club Constitution – and now the fun begins! Everyone will have their own ideas about which shares to buy. There will be cautious members who want to minimise risk by buying FT-SE 100 listed companies only, or even just unit or investment trusts. Then there will be those who want to risk it all on penny shares which might double or even treble in value. There may even be members who want to dabble in share options and futures, where rewards and risks can be dramatic. But it's wise to err on the side of caution. Build a portfolio of good quality shares first, and then set aside a percentage of the club's income for riskier investments.

4. Invest wisely through your club – remember, the golden rules of profitable investing still apply. Never invest more than you can afford to lose.

Shares can go down as well as up, and the collapse in hi-tech share prices this spring hurt investors who'd invested more than they had to spare. Be savvy – use your existing knowledge to help you make profitable investments. For example, if you work as a chemist then look at news about pharmaceutical companies. Your understanding of this sector will help you spot potential winners. Also look to develop your knowledge and understanding of how the stock market works – use reputable information sources with proven track records to help you. Your club could split the cost of subscription between each member. After everyone has expressed their opinion at the weekly or monthly meeting, a vote is taken on which shares to buy or sell.

5. Remember to have fun! Investment clubs aren't just about making money. Meetings are normally accompanied by a few drinks and choosing the latest investment is often preceded by heated debate and a few (usually) good humoured 'I told you so's'. The important thing is that everyone has their say before a vote. The Cranham Investment Club from Gloucestershire, for instance, has been running for over 3 years and won The ProShare Investment Club of the Year in 1999. This group of villagers came together through their parish magazine. In addition to profiting from their investment policy, the club provides a focus for life in the village. They meet monthly in the local pub, and the club is made up of people with backgrounds as diverse as engineering, farming, nursing, photography, teaching and telecommunications.

Bottom Line: Whether you are an experienced investor or an absolute beginner you can benefit from membership of an investment club. Your knowledge and experience will increase and you can bounce your ideas off other members. Experienced investors find an investment club a good way to share their hobby with friends and gain ideas for their own portfolios. Also, in time, new investors will use the knowledge they gain through an investment club to begin an individual portfolio of their own. Knowledge is shared between members and even those new to investing will almost certainly have an opinion about companies and sectors from their experience in work, leisure and life generally. Everyone has something to contribute and everyone can learn something.

THE BEST TIME TO BET ON FOOTBALL MATCHES

PFC tip: last-minute betting is often most advantageous. Why: odds that are set in advance on fixed odds coupons cannot take account of late changes and developments such as managerial resignations, dismissals and injuries to key players. This can give shrewd punters an edge over the bookmakers.

HEALTH

EAT MORE – BUT WEIGH LESS

Many people stick to a calorie-controlled, fat-counted meal plan for months, but eventually return to their old eating habits – and find the pounds pile back on again. But it doesn't have to be like this if you adopt a different approach. Here are the dos and don'ts for success:

1. **Eat more high carbohydrates** – bread, potatoes, pasta, rice and cereals. These provide starch and fibre. Base your diet around these foods but avoid smothering them with butter, cream sauces and/or mayonnaise. Fruit and vegetables are low in calories and high in vitamins, minerals and dietary fibre. Vegetables should be eaten raw or cooked lightly to retain their nutrients. Also eat more protein – most concentrated in meat, fish, poultry, nuts, beans, lentils and peas. White fish is particularly nutritious and low in calories; include it three times a week. Avoid fattier meats, or trim off all the fat. Dairy products are the main source of calcium although many have a high fat content. Choose lower-fat options – cottage cheese, yoghurt, skimmed milk. Water is an essential part of any diet. It works as a purifier, flushing toxins out of the body. And if you have a glass of water before a meal, it can stop you over-eating by making you feel full sooner. Try fizzy mineral water to help satisfy cravings for sugary drinks.

2. **Eat less fat.** Substitute high-fat dairy products for low-fat alternatives.

Use low-fat cooking methods – grilling, boiling, steaming. Reduce your sugar intake – from pastries, chocolate and sweets. Eating sweet things only after meals is helpful. Cut back on salt – your body requires only small amounts. Adding salt to our food can mean that we are taking in as much as 1000% more than the body needs; and can lead to high blood pressure. Avoid salting your meals, and cut down on processed foods, which contain a high amount of salt. Alcohol has no fat, but contains lots of calories. Health Authority guide: half a pint of bitter has 90 calories, ordinary strength lager has 85; a measure of spirits has 50; a glass of wine has 75 calories.

3. Change your lifestyle. Amending lifelong habits takes time and patience. So, introduce new foods on a step-by-step basis. Even eating a small piece of fruit a day, going without cream on strawberries, or grilling when you used to fry, is a positive beginning. Examine your lifestyle. Do you work long hours? If so, you could be snacking on high-fat foods – so start by choosing fast food that is low in fat, such as bananas or popcorn. Are you stressed at work? It's likely that you could be overeating to compensate – being aware of this is a good start. Do you have to entertain people at work? You might be eating two big meals a day instead of the usual one. Miss out one of the lunchtime courses and choose healthier options from the menu. Try new recipes out on your family; but note that children need more fat in their diets than adults do. Also, take more exercise – a 20-minute walk helps burn off the calories of a big meal.

Bottom line: once you've started your healthy eating plan, you'll soon realise that the food is really delicious. Follow the Mediterranean cuisine of southern Italy, France and Spain: those countries that are famous for their culinary expertise and with diets that consist primarily of bread, pasta, rice, and vegetables. Most of their recipes are easy-to-follow and quick-to-produce. And the reduced rates of heart disease and strokes in those countries are thought to be due to the local diets.

WAKE UP WITHOUT A HANGOVER

PFC tip: the best way to handle a hangover is to prevent it happening in the first place. Alcohol is a diuretic – it flushes away the water in your body and causes you to dehydrate. It also causes you to lose the body's natural supply of water-soluble vitamins and minerals. And it is this mixture of dehydration and vitamin and mineral deficiency that makes you feel so awful. As an alternative, avoid drinking on an empty stomach, have an occasional glass of water when you're drinking alcohol, and drink lots of water before going to sleep. Also take a dose of vitamin C and a vitamin B complex or brewer's yeast tablets or multivitamin supplements – and stop a hangover in its tracks. The best drinks to order to avoid a hangover are gin and vodka.

HOW TO PREVENT A DISEASE THAT AFFECTS 33% OF THE POPULATION

Candida albicans is the little-known but major disease of the 21st century. Its symptoms include drowsiness, frequent infections, skin problems, feelings of anxiety and irritability. And cravings for chocolate, sugary cereal, bread and/or alcohol, digestive problems, weak muscles, mood swings or depression, pains in the chest, dizziness and/or urinary infections. You'll be particularly susceptible if you've taken lots of antibiotics in the past – over-prescription is the major cause of the disease. As a preventative measure always make sure that any treatment is absolutely necessary before you agree to take any course of antibiotics – you may be able to transform your health simply by reducing your intake of antibiotics.

SURGERY-FREE FACELIFTS AND TEN VALUABLE TIPS TO COMBAT THE EFFECTS OF AGE

Growing older is inevitable, but there are many ways of holding back time and looking your best. You can appear ten years younger by following these facial tips – and you'll feel fitter and healthier as well.

1. Cleanse and moisturise your face daily with products which are suited to your skin type – men should do this too. Your facial skin is only around 0.12mm thick and very delicate. Make sure you don't forget to use a rich moisturiser on your neck – this area is most prone to crinkly skin that is an instant age giveaway.

2. Drink lots of water each day. About 70% of the body is made up of water; and it's vital to your skin's wellbeing. Drink at least one litre a day to help keep your face looking fresh and radiant.

3. Stay pale. It is important to protect your facial skin every day with a UVA sunscreen – even in the dullest weather. Without this protection, ultraviolet radiation will cause wrinkles.

4. Treat your face to a good diet. Eat lots of fresh fruit, vegetables and whole grains. These will provide your skin with all the vitamins and nutrients it needs to stay healthy. Avoid caffeine, white sugar and convenience foods that damage your skin.

5. Give up smoking immediately. The evil weed uses up valuable vitamin C in the body. As a consequence, your skin will have more wrinkles than non-smokers' and will look yellow.

6. Go without make-up every now and again. This gives your skin a chance to breathe. Also combine this with a brisk walk or cycle ride in the fresh air to bring a healthy glow to your cheeks.

7. Invest in an electronic muscle stimulator for a surgery-free 'face lift'. EMS machines work by stimulating muscles to contract and relax as they do during normal exercise. It's painless and convenient – the machine does all of the exercising for you.

8. Enjoy yourself. Smiling and laughing exercises your face with minimal effort, and keeps it taut and healthy. And a smiling face always appears more attractive than a sullen or worried-looking one.

9. De-stress your life – this will help your face to cut down on its worry lines. It's a fact – happy people look younger! And be sure you get enough beauty sleep as regular rest gives your skin cells a chance to regenerate.

PFC beauty secrets: a lightly beaten egg white mixed with two teaspoons of cornflour makes a cheap and effective face mask. Alternatively mix together a mashed-up banana with a tablespoon of honey, and apply for 20 minutes. Egg white is also a good treatment for open pores. Adding sunflower oil to warm water can help to soften your skin. Treat tired eyes by holding a peeled and grated raw potato against them. Or use cold, wet teabags for a similar rejuvenating effect. Petroleum jelly removes mascara well, and also thickens eyelashes.

EAT THE FOODS YOUR BLOOD NEEDS TO HELP COMBAT STRESS, HEART DISEASE AND CANCER

There are literally thousands of diets. Some claim to make you thinner or younger-looking, whilst others promise to make you healthier and allergy-free. They all work on the false premise that one diet suits all. Now a diet has been developed which caters for the individual. Devised by US doctor, Peter D' Adamo, The Eat Right Diet is a programme which comes in four varieties – A, B, O and AB. It's not based on calories, or food groups but on blood types. He claims that knowing and working with your blood group will enable you to lose weight, avoid chronic disease, enjoy longevity, physical vitality and emotional strength.

How can your blood type have such an impact on your health and weight? There is a chemical reaction between your blood and the foods you eat – this process is what makes up your individual personal chemistry. It's fundamental to health and weight loss because each blood group reacts differently from the other. Your individual blood type determines the way you absorb nutrients, how you interact with food, handle stress and exercise most efficiently. The connection between blood type, disease and diet is not another new diet fad to hit the market – in the 1950s researchers linked diseases such as stomach cancer, peptic ulcers, rheumatism and urinary tract infections to specific blood groups. Each blood group holds the blueprint of how you evolved and knowing how to use that information is the basis of good health. Environment and natural selection determined the diets of our ancestors, which is why certain diets work for some and not for others and why certain blood types are more susceptible to specific illnesses.

Make the diet work for you – discover your blood type to maximise your health. If you don't have a record of your blood type ask your doctor or the blood transfusion service, if you give blood. If you don't, this is a good opportunity to potentially save someone's life in addition to finding out your blood group. Most GP's surgeries will do the test for you, but can charge a fee of up to £30. Some health supplement companies also offer blood testing. Higher Nature offer a mail-order service for £6, phone them for more information on 01435 882880. Once you know your blood type you'll then be able to discover which food and drinks you should be consuming and those to avoid, in addition to what supplements you should be taking and the best exercise regime to follow. All blood types can have foods from the various groups outlined below, but there are specific foods within each group that are better suited to your body's needs. Once you know your blood group, this is what your diet could look like:

Type O – this is the oldest and most common blood type, dating back to the Cro-Magnons. Our first ancestors were hunters and this dictated the kind of digestion this group developed. Your typical characteristics are: meat-eater; hardy digestive tract; overactive immune system; intolerance to dietary and environmental adaptations; you require an efficient metabolism to stay lean and healthy; and respond best to stress with intense physical activity. This group had the most limited access to food types – which is why it now has the simplest and most restricted diet. It's based on a high protein intake, mostly from meat, with small amounts of carbohydrate. You must cut out wheat and most other grains. Foods that encourage weight loss for this blood group include kelp and seafood, red meat, liver, spinach, broccoli and kale. Foods that encourage weight gain include wheat, gluten, sweetcorn, cabbage, Brussels sprouts and cauliflower. To physically thrive and avoid stress, take vigorous aerobic exercise. This blood type increases your chances of developing ulcers and inflammatory diseases.

Type A – the next blood group to develop, were the cultivators. This blood group adapted in response to a more domestic and settled lifestyle. Your characteristics are: the first vegetarians; sensitive digestive tract; tolerant immune system; adapt well to settled dietary and environmental conditions; respond best to stress with calming action; require agrarian diet to stay lean and productive. This 'second stage' diet is ideally based on a high carbohydrate and low fat intake. This group does best with a vegetarian diet. Foods that encourage weight loss include vegetable oils and soya foods, vegetables and pineapple. Foods that encourage weight gain include meat, dairy foods, kidney beans and wheat in large amounts. Less rigorous exercise such as yoga or golf is ideal. You best release stress by meditating. This blood group is at increased risk of acquiring cancer and heart disease.

Type B – the nomadic part of our history. This blood group's ancestors were from the tribes that migrated north from Africa to Europe, Asia and the Americas. Your characteristics are: balanced; strong immune system; tolerant digestive system; most flexible dietary choices; dairy eater; respond best to stress with creativity; and require a balance between physical and mental activity to stay lean and sharp. This group thrives on a varied diet, including meat and dairy products. Foods that encourage weight loss include green vegetables, meat, liver, eggs and liquorice tea (do not take liquorice in supplement form without your doctor's consent). Foods that encourage weight gain include sweetcorn, lentils, peanuts, sesame seeds and buckwheat. Moderate exercise such as swimming or walking is ideal both for health and stress reduction. This blood group is at increased risk of acquiring slow-growing viruses that attack the nervous system.

Type AB – this could be best identified as the adaptor blood type. This is the newest and rarest blood group which appeared around 1,000-1,500AD. It is believed to be a response to the intermingling of the blood groups on a major scale, with the sweep through Asia and across Europe by Genghis Khan and his armies. Your characteristics are: chameleon response to changing environmental and dietary conditions; sensitive digestive tract; excessively tolerant immune system; respond best to stress spiritually, with both physical and creative energy. Because this group adapted last, it combines the benefits and tolerances of both groups A and B so has a varied diet with few restrictions. Foods that encourage weight loss include tofu, seafood, kelp, green vegetables, dairy products, alkaline fruits and pineapple. Foods that encourage weight gain include red meat, kidney beans, seeds, sweetcorn and buckwheat. Calming exercises such as T'ai Chi and yoga work best for stress and fitness for this group. This blood group has an increased risk factor for most illnesses – as you have the most 'friendly' immune system of all blood groups that lets in most diseases.

Bottom Line: The Eat Right Diet is highly effective in raising energy levels and initiating weight loss. The greatest benefit is that it's a 'diet for life' that you can adapt to become your everyday recipe for healthy living. You can banish fad or yo-yo diets for good, with the bonus of knowing that if you eat 'right' for your blood type you may also help prevent serious and chronic illnesses from developing.

SIMPLE EXERCISES FOR PERFECT EYESIGHT – AT ANY AGE

Many eye-related problems are caused by eyestrain. This happens when the eye strains to see something and the muscles surrounding it become tense and rigid. These then put pressure on the eyeball and distort its shape. But here's some good news – we can train ourselves to relax these muscles completely and make related eyesight problems disappear. Here is a simple and easy-to-follow series of regular exercises designed to help the eye muscles relax – they should be performed without glasses or contact lenses.

1. Eye lines: keeping your head relaxed and still, allow your eyes to move up and down six times. Avoid any strain or effort. Repeat this three times, with a few seconds of rest in between. Then repeat – this time moving the eyes from left to right and back again. This exercise helps relax the stiff, strained muscles around the eyes.

2. Palming: sit in a comfortable chair and gently rest the palms of both hands over your closed eyes. Remain like this for about ten minutes. Remove your hands and open your eyes. Now try to pick out objects of one particular colour, choosing a different colour for every day of the week.

3. Butterfly blinking: blink quickly for a few seconds, then gently squeeze your eyelids shut for a moment. Repeat the exercise for up to a minute. This exercise shifts the point of focus of the eye, and also helps to lubricate the outer surface by stimulating the tear ducts.

4. Tracing shapes: imagine there is a pencil extending from the tip of your nose. Use this to trace the outline of various objects about you, some near and others further away. This exercise helps to strengthen the ability of the eye to focus on objects at different distances. Vary the exercise by tracing figures of eight in the air.

5. Swinging: this should be practised standing up, but can be done sitting down. Relax your neck, and gently swing your head from side to side, backwards and forwards. Swinging is designed to relax the neck and shoulder muscles and improve the blood supply to the eyes. It is important that all of these exercises are performed in a relaxed and rhythmical way, without any strain or jerkiness. It can be helpful to put on relaxing music while you are doing them. To gain most benefit from the exercises they need to be performed regularly; at least once a day.

Bonus: combine these five natural exercises with other ways of improving your eyesight. To ensure your eyes are nourished properly, eat plenty of fresh fruit, vegetables and high-fibre foods (wholemeal bread, nuts, fruit), and cut down on fatty foods, sugar and salt. If you suffer from poor vision at night, try increasing your vitamin A intake – from fish, carrots, tomatoes and spinach. Exercise stimulates your blood flow, bringing more oxygen and fuel to the eyes and taking away waste products. This is a proven way of reducing stress and helping you to relax. Eyes thrive on natural daylight, so when reading or doing close-up work, position yourself near to a window. Avoid wearing dark glasses indoors or in normal daylight, unless they have been prescribed for a medical condition. If you have to work in artificial light, try to avoid fluorescent strip lighting, especially when it flickers. Ordinary light bulbs are better. Full spectrum strip lights and artificial daylight bulbs are best.

Bottom line: laser eye surgery is becoming increasingly popular. The most common procedure is called Photorefractive Keratectomy (PRK) and involves reshaping the outer surface of the eye with surgical lasers. Lasers are computer-calibrated and directed with pinpoint accuracy; and their beams do not penetrate beyond the surface of the eye. So, surgery is safe and painless. It is only suitable for people with mild to moderate short-sightedness. People with long-sight and anyone under 21 years should avoid it as their eyesight is still changing. There is no upper age limit for the treatment, although it may be inappropriate for people with certain medical conditions. Always check with your GP before applying for laser eye surgery.

How: initially, you will be asked to attend a consultation for a thorough eye examination and a discussion about the operation with the surgeon. On the day of the operation, the eye will be anaesthetised with drops; no injection is required. The operation itself takes only a few minutes and is pain-free. After there may be some discomfort as the outer surface of the eye heals. But side effects normally last for no more than a few days. Eyesight can take a few weeks to stabilise fully – and driving a car or operating machinery is strictly forbidden during this time. Also as PRK involves removing part of the outer surface of the eye, your eyes may always be a little more sensitive than they were before. For example, it may no longer be possible to wear contact lenses (if you still need them) after the surgery. The more short-sighted you are, the greater the chance of such side effects arising. It's crucial to ask specifically about these potential dangers before the operation is carried out.

Important: laser eye surgery is performed on one eye at a time; the other eye will be treated three to six months later. Many people no longer need glasses after the operation. Others experience an improvement, but still need glasses some or all of the time. The exact results cannot be predicted; much depends on how your eyes respond to the treatment. PRK will not reverse the normal effects of ageing, in particular the need for reading glasses in older people. This type of surgery is not normally available on the NHS, so you will have to pay a fee. Clinics advertise in local and national newspapers; your GP and optician should be able to help you make your choice. Contact several different clinics, and speak to people who have been treated there before reaching a decision.

A PROVEN HERBAL REMEDY FOR A PERFECT NIGHT'S SLEEP

PFC tip: a very effective over-the-counter herbal remedy for insomnia is 'Passiflora Lehning' drops. Ingredients include avena sativa, passiflora, belladonna, secale and valerian. Recent UK laboratory tests show that the herb valerian alone helped 44% of insomniacs to get 'a perfect night's sleep', whilst a staggering 89% reported 'improved sleep'.

DON'T LOSE YOUR TEETH TO THE DISEASE THAT AFFECTS 50% OF THE POPULATION

Follow these two simple instructions to dramatically cut your chances of suffering from gum disease. 1: Treat your teeth to a deep clean at regular intervals to reach and destroy the inaccessible bacteria missed by normal, everyday brushing. Wet your toothbrush in hydrogen peroxide. Dip its bristles into a baking soda and salt mixture. Brush this over your teeth and gums, making sure that you include the spaces between your teeth. Leave the mixture to soak in for two minutes. 2: Rinse thoroughly. Top up your calcium intake whenever you can; a deficiency of this vital mineral can weaken your teeth and increase the chances of gum infection. Sources: low-fat milk, green leafy vegetables, legumes, salmon, low-fat yoghurt.

FLATTEN YOUR STOMACH IN JUST THREE MONTHS

Having a flat stomach improves your posture, strengthens your back and makes you less susceptible to injury and illness. It will improve your appearance too. And if you look good, you'll feel great. Unfortunately, modern living encourages weak muscles and a sagging stomach. But you can do something about it. Here's how:

Concentrate on the four muscle groups that support your stomach – upper abdominals, lower abdominals, external oblique, internal oblique. Details: the upper and lower abdominals are on the front of the abdomen and form a row of muscles that runs from the ribs to the pubic bone. When they are well developed they are oblong in shape. the top half comprises the upper abdominals and the bottom half includes the lower abdominals. The external and internal obliques are not as easy to see as the abdominals, but are equally important. They form two bands of muscles that stretch down either side of your body, between your abdomen and waist. They run from the bottom of your ribs to the top of your hips. The internal oblique lies underneath the external oblique. Before starting any of these exercises, avoid any strain or injury to your muscles by doing this simple warm-up:

Upper body warm-up: Stand up as straight as possible and place your arms above your head. Then hold this position for five seconds, and lower your arms so they're outstretched by your side. Again, hold this position for five seconds. Then swing your arms so they're outstretched in front of you – and hold for five seconds. Do all three arm movements at least three times each.

Lower body warm-up: Lie down on your left side in a straight line with your right leg resting on the left one. Next gently lift your upper leg about 12 inches above your lower leg and make a small circular movement with your foot. And after each circle, lower your leg again and repeat up to five times. Then turn over, lie on your other side and repeat the exercise with your left leg.

Basic starting position: lie flat on your back, keeping your knees together and your feet flat on the floor. Bend your knees upwards at an angle of 90 degrees. Press your lower back into the floor. Place your arms flat by your sides. Do practise getting into this position and familiarise yourself with it.

Exercise 1: from the starting position, place your hands flat under your hips, palm side down. Keep your knees bent and your legs together. Brace your abdominal muscles. Bring your legs up until they are at right angles to your body. Use your abdominals to pull your knees towards your chest. Hold this position for two seconds, then repeat.

Exercise 2: from the starting position, keep your knees bent and your legs together. Brace your abdominal muscles. Slowly pull your knees towards your chest. Unfold your legs gradually and point them straight towards the ceiling. Keep your legs and feet pressed together. Rotate your legs slowly in a very small circle, about four inches in each direction. Do half the repetitions clockwise, and the other half anti-clockwise. Bend your knees again before lowering your legs.

Exercise 3: from the starting position, place your hands behind your head. Tuck your chin on to your chest. Press your lower back into the floor. Tighten your abdominal muscles and your buttocks. Breathe in. Breathe out slowly, at the same time raising your head and shoulders until they are a third of the way off the floor. Hold this position for one second, then return gently to the starting position. Never raise your body more than 30 degrees – a third of the way – off the floor. Your abdominal muscles are only capable of lifting you this far and if you raise yourself any higher, your spine will have to do most of the work. This does nothing to help your muscles and could damage your back. Do the exercise slowly and feel your abdominals working. Don't try to raise yourself higher by bouncing, nor by using the momentum you gain from that return movement. Use only your abdominal muscles, and try to 'unroll' yourself off the floor.

Exercise 4: from the starting position, bring your knees towards your chest. Keep your knees bent, and your legs in the air. Your thighs must be vertical; and your lower legs should be horizontal. Place your hands behind your head. Tuck your chin on to your chest. Breathe in. Breathe out slowly, keeping your legs in the same position and raising your head and shoulders a third of the way off the floor. Hold the position momentarily. Lower your head and shoulders, but keep your legs in the same position all the time. Repeat the exercise if you feel good.

Exercise 5: from the starting position, brace your abdominal muscles and your buttocks. Place your hands behind your head. Tuck your chin on to your chest. Breathe in. Breathe out slowly whilst slowly raising your left shoulder and your left hip off the floor. Hold the position for one second then return to the starting position. Repeat the exercise for the other side.

Beginners' routine: warm up; exercise 1 – five repetitions; exercise 3 – five repetitions; exercise 4 – five repetitions; cool down. Continue this for a few sessions until it becomes easy; and then move up to ten repetitions. When you feel comfortable with ten repetitions, move up to 15 repetitions. When that becomes easy, go on to do the intermediate routine.

Intermediate routine: warm up; exercise 1 – 20 repetitions; exercise 2 – 20 repetitions; exercise 3 – 20 repetitions; exercise 4 – 20 repetitions; cool down. Continue this for a few days and then move up to 25 repetitions. And when you are comfortable with 25, go on to the advanced routine.

Advanced routine: warm up; exercise 1 – 30 repetitions; exercise 2 – 30 repetitions; exercise 3 – 30 repetitions; exercise 4 – 30 repetitions; exercise 5 – 30 repetitions; cool down. This is designed to work the obliques, the lower abdominals, and the upper abdominals. You only need to do the exercises every other day – the abdominals tone up better when you rest them between sessions; but try to do some aerobic exercise every day. Reminder: do consult your doctor before starting an exercise programme if you are overweight, and/or have a back problem, and/or have any special medical needs, and/or don't exercise regularly.

YOUR COMPREHENSIVE GUIDE TO CONQUERING BACK PAIN

Back pain can come on in a couple of hours, take weeks to subside, and just when you think it is better, it returns, twice as painful as before. Almost as frustrating is the way that some doctors look at your back, prescribe painkillers and tell you, 'there's nothing you can do about back pain'. But this is simply not true. Medical practitioners of various kinds can treat back pain successfully, and by changing your habits, you can do even more than they can to prevent it recurring. Here are the prevention techniques taught by Britain's top private specialists:

Standing: stand tall, but don't be too rigid about it. Important: distribute the weight of your body evenly to each foot. Bend your knees very slightly and pull in the base of your spine. A good exercise is to hold up a book in front of your face until you feel your head tilting backwards slightly and your eyes gazing slightly downwards.

Walking: aim for a 'military bearing', with your shoulders back, chest forward and stomach in. But do not lean forward. It can be helpful, when walking, to consciously stretch your back all the way up to your neck. Avoid sudden changes of direction, especially ones that involve twisting your trunk. And choose suitable footwear – the limp caused by a blister or a corn from an ill-fitting shoe can throw your back out of alignment.

Lifting: never bend over when lifting a heavy object. Avoid using your back; let your legs do the work, because your leg muscles are far stronger than your back muscles. If possible, break down the load into smaller pieces. Get as close to the object as possible. Place your feet either side of it. Bend your knees and squat down, keeping your back straight. Grasp the object firmly and stand up by straightening your knees.

Sitting: choose a well-designed chair – one that is firm, rather than softly-upholstered. It is essential to sit on a flat, horizontal seat that meets the back of the chair at a right angle or more. The chair should be a height that enables your hips and knees to bend at right angles and your feet to rest on the ground. For a person of average height, the seat should be 18-19 inches off the ground. It's important that the back should be at least as high as your shoulder blades, and the arms at least seven inches above the seat. To sit properly, push the base of your spine into the back of the chair. Use a small, sausage-shaped cushion or a rolled-up towel to support your back, if necessary. Don't sit in the same position for too long. When getting up from an easy chair, support as much of your body weight as you can by grasping the arms of the chair. Your office chair should allow you to sit with your back straight and your forearms resting on the desk. For a person of average height, the seat should be about 18-19 inches high, with the desk at about 27- 28 inches from the floor. If you're going to be typing most of the time, have the desk about two inches lower than this.

Driving: ideally, the seat should be firmly-sprung, with side sections that provide lateral support. It should extend as far forward as the back of your calves (at least 21 inches) and be 11-12 inches above your heels when they're using the pedals. Key fact: the higher the back of the seat, the better. Fit a head-rest if you can. And a lumbar support cushion will improve any car seat too. If you spend a lot of time driving, it's probably worth buying an orthopaedic seat designed specially for you. On long journeys, stop the car, get out and walk around at least every two hours.

Sleeping: if you wake up with back pain, your bed is probably too soft. If the mattress is sagging in the middle, buy a new, firmer one – ideally, pick an orthopaedic one that is designed specially for your condition. If the bed is sagging, put boards or even an old door under the mattress; making sure that this support stretches from the head to the foot of the bed. Alternatively try putting the mattress on the floor. Your sleeping position is also important – sleep flat on your back without a pillow and take extra care when getting in and out of bed.

YOGA FOR BEGINNERS – A STEP-BY-STEP GUIDE TO A STRESS-FREE LIFE

'Yoga' means 'union' – and involves the linking of our physical, emotional, intellectual and spiritual powers into a single holistic approach. Yoga is designed to free and develop the whole person in us and is achieved through three basic techniques – developing the body through physical exercise or postures (asana), controlling the will and emotions through correct breathing (pranayama), and freeing the mind through meditation techniques (dharana). Here's how it can work and make you a more complete person:

Neck and shoulder exercises: 1. Sit up straight on a hard-backed chair. Look to the front and breathe in through the nose. Slowly turn your head to the right; at the same time breathe out. Breathe in, moving your head back to the front. Breathe out, moving your head to the left this time; and so on. Repeat the exercise several times. 2. Repeat the first exercise; this time moving your head down on the out-breath so your chin rests on your chest; and dropping your head back for the second part of the exercise. 3. Breathe in, at the same time holding your arms straight up above your head whilst throwing back your head. Breathe out, swinging your arms and head down to the front, with your head ending up between your knees. Repeat six or seven times. Always breathe through your nose rather than your mouth.

Stretch and twist exercises: these loosen up the rest of your muscles. 1. Stand straight with your feet close together and join your hands in a prayer position on your chest. Retain this position for two minutes. Then lift your arms – still in the prayer position – above your head and straighten them; at the same time breathing in. Breathe out, dropping your arms. Repeat this arm-lifting exercise five or six times. 2. Lift your arms again; but this time hold your hands apart above your head. Stretch them forward towards your toes, breathing out. Breathe in, straighten your back, and stretch your arms straight back above your head. Repeat the exercise several times. 3. Repeat the second exercise; but this time stretch your arms to the left, and then to the right. Keep your torso to the front. 4. Lower your arms and gently swing them left to right – one arm at the front, one behind – whilst twisting your body.

Spine and back exercises: a correctly aligned spine and supple back are important features of yoga practice. 1. Sit up straight on the floor. Keep your legs straight out in front and lift your arms straight up above your head, whilst breathing in. Breathe out and try to touch your feet or calves; whilst keeping your arms and legs as straight as possible. Breathing in and out, hold this position for 30 seconds. 2. Lie face down on the floor with your hands by your sides. Breathe in and lift your head, bringing your arms straight out to the front to support you. Hold this position for 30 seconds whilst breathing in and out; and coming back down on an out-breath. It is important that yoga postures are balanced. If you stretch one way, always stretch the other way to compensate.

Health: yoga doesn't just tone you up and keep you fit. These exercises have therapeutic effects on all parts of your body. It can alleviate or even remedy such problems as arthritis, asthma, back pain, constipation, headaches, heart, kidney and liver complaints, hypertension, insomnia, psoriasis and varicose veins. For example, the shoulder stand – 'sarvangasana' – is good for poor blood circulation, nervous disorders, stomach, abdominal and urinary complaints, throat and nasal ailments. A balanced diet will also enhance the health benefits of yoga. If you have any problems that affect your health in any way, always check with your doctor before starting a yoga course.

Stress: yoga offers many exercises that reduce body tension and help to alleviate stress. 1. On hearing bad news, sit quietly with a straight back and place your hands on your chest. Try to slow your breathing, feeling the breath expanding and deflating your lungs in the process. 2. If you feel worried, place your fingertips on your forehead and consciously slow down your breathing, making it as quiet as possible. 3. If you're feeling irritable, place your hands on your chest in a prayer position. Close your eyes and breath calmly and slowly.

Deep-seated stress: a regular series of postures controlled by nasal breathing may be necessary. 1. Lie on your back with your legs arched up and separated, and with the feet just below the buttocks. Spread your arms out to either side of your body so that you form a 'T' shape. Breathe in and out slowly, letting your weight sink into the floor as you exhale. Do this for five minutes. 2. Staying on your back, fold your legs up and wrap your arms around the back of your thighs. Hold this position for two minutes. 3. Sit back on your heels. Tuck your head between your knees, letting your arms hang loosely behind you alongside of your legs. Breathe in and out; slowly and easily. 4. Stand up straight with your arms by your side and your feet hip-distance apart. Perform that third neck and shoulder exercise. 5. Adopt the shoulder stand, followed by the corpse posture. It's best to practise this sequence of five exercises twice a day in addition to your normal yoga practice.

Relaxation: yoga is a flexible form of discipline, and can be practised in small or large ways; at home or at work, for a minute or for an hour. Typical: a few simple stretching exercises can relieve stress in the office – a consequence of being hunched over a computer all morning. 1. Sit up straight and link your fingers together at the back of your head. Take a deep breath and breathe out, bringing the chin down to the top of your chest and drawing the elbows closer together. Hold the position, breathe in again and then release. Repeat this four or five times. 2. Sit up straight and breathe in. Then stretch your arms above your head linking your fingers together so that the palms of your hands are facing the ceiling. Hold this position before breathing out and bringing your arms down slowly. Repeat the exercise four or five times.

WHY YOUR DENTAL FILLINGS COULD BE MAKING YOU ILL

Evidence is mounting that mercury dental fillings could be a major factor in more than 30 medical conditions. ME, Multiple Sclerosis, Alzheimer's, infertility, headaches, stomach problems and allergies – they've all been linked with those silvery metal fillings. In tests on immunity it has been revealed that the number of T-cells – vital to successful immunity – are increased by up to 300% when amalgam fillings are removed. While many dentists disdain the recent anti-mercury hysteria, the dental profession seems to be moving away from mercury fillings and using alternative materials.

PFC remedy: if you're worried that your fillings may be causing health problems, you can have a simple test to determine whether or not they are making you ill. If so, you can have them removed. Information: the British Society for Mercury-Free Dentistry, 020 7373 3655.

WHY DRINKING COFFEE CAN BE GOOD FOR YOU

Coffee has had a bad press in recent years, and is subject to many myths. But the reality is that the latest worldwide research has shown that there is little or no evidence that drinking coffee in moderation is likely to create any health hazards for most people. In fact, coffee can bring some very definite health benefits, according to recent medical studies. Let's look at the myths and reality:

Myth: the plain and simple fact is that many of the ill effects commonly associated with coffee are just not true. In particular: 'Drinking coffee harms your heart'. Researchers involved in a massive study in America concluded that 'any suggestion of a positive association between heart disease and coffee is eliminated'. Source: *Journal of the American Medical Association.*

'Coffee causes palpitations', those uncomfortable flutters that occur now and again in even the healthiest people. The new research is categorical in its findings: GPs should not tell patients suffering from palpitations to cut down on coffee. Source: consultants at the Royal Infirmary, Edinburgh, Scotland, following a study to establish whether or not there was any link between coffee and palpitations.

'Drinking coffee adversely affects your blood pressure and heartbeat'. Reports on caffeine releasing natural body chemicals that affect blood pressure and heartbeat show that these effects are found only when caffeine is taken in sizeable amounts by people who normally never consume it. The effects are not found in those who drink coffee on a regular basis. Source: *Heart*, the specialist medical journal.

Reality: telling someone to stop drinking coffee is just taking away one of the pleasures of life for no sound reason. There are numerous benefits:

Coffee boosts the brain. It helps you to think more quickly, have a better memory and improves reasoning powers. This increase in mental performance is more marked in older people than in younger ones. Source: *Psychopharmacology.*

It increases energy and endurance. Strong coffee helps people work longer and harder and stave off exhaustion; the caffeine stimulates the body's energy reserves. Sources: *International Journal of Sports Medicine, Canadian Journal of Applied Physiology*. Drinking two cups of coffee before a night shift can be as helpful for staving off sleepiness as having a nap before starting work. Sources: *Sleep, Neuropsychobiology.*

Coffee can minimise cold symptoms. The after-effects of a cold can affect your moods, hand-eye co-ordination and reaction times, but a cup of coffee can produce a 'feel-good' factor that gives you a lift and reduces some of these sluggish symptoms. Source: *University of Bristol Newsletter.*

It can limit feelings of depression – those feelings that, left unchecked, can even lead to an increased risk of suicide. A ten-year survey of 86,000 nurses found that those who drank coffee were less likely to commit suicide than those who did not. Source: *Archives of Internal Medicine*. And this finding supports a ten-year follow-up of 128,000 in a medical care programme that discovered that the chance of death by suicide dropped as people drank more coffee. Source: *Annals of Epidemiology*.

Coffee can help cut road accidents; a coffee break could make the difference between life and death for drivers. Drivers falling asleep at the wheel cause one in five of all road accidents in Britain. Researchers say that caffeine helps to keep people alert and vigilant while on the road. Source: *British Medical Journal*.

Coffee may have a protective effect. A study of 10,000 people in Scotland found that those who did not drink coffee at all had a significantly higher rate of heart diseases than coffee drinkers. Source: '*Journal of Epidemiology and Community Health*.'

Bottom line: This exhaustive research shows that coffee presents no great risk to health, providing it is drunk in moderation. But different coffees contain varying amounts of caffeine – 80-90mg in a standard (150ml) cup of ground coffee; 60mg in a standard cup of instant coffee; and just 3mg in a standard cup of decaffeinated coffee. Work out your own intake of caffeine based on the type of coffee you drink. Researchers also agree that people who drink coffee – and other caffeine-containing drinks – do not become dependent or addicted to it.

HAPPINESS

CHANGE YOUR DIET AND CHEER YOURSELF UP

PFC tip: mounting evidence shows that depression and even schizophrenia can sometimes be caused by nothing more than dietary deficiencies or food allergies. An Italian study revealed that almost all of the 331 depressed people taking part in the test had extremely low levels of cholesterol in their body. Evidence shows that very low-fat diets can cause depression. And insufficient levels of B vitamins, high intakes of sugar and caffeine, and gluten or milk allergies have all been shown to cause or aggravate mental illness too. Your doctor won't tell you that other common triggers for depression include some prescription drugs such as antihistamines, antibiotics, drugs for high blood pressure, nasal decongestants and heart drugs. The last thing you want to deal with when you're suffering from depression is an episode of ill health. But that's exactly what you can experience with many common depression drugs. Tricyclic antidepressants can cause delirium, fatigue, excessive sweating, the dangerous lowering of blood pressure, and even strokes and heart attacks. Prozac has brought on vomiting, diarrhoea, anxiety, insomnia, sexual problems, muscle, bone, ear and eye pain and even suicide in some people.

HOW TO BE THE LIFE AND SOUL OF EVERY PARTY

From ice breakers to party entertainments – here are our favourite party games that will make you the toast of any party. Simple to arrange and play, these fun games will guarantee that your name will appear on the guest list of every party for years to come!

WHO AM I?

Equipment: Paper, pen, and pins

Preparation: A list of famous people – anyone from Tony Blair to Lily Savage or Bart Simpson!

As your guests arrive, pin one name from your list on each of their backs. Each guest must then find out who they are by asking the other players questions such as "Am I an actor? Am I a comedian?" The only answer that can be given is "yes" or "no", and each guest may only ask three questions before moving on.

It doesn't matter if some guests figure out who they are long before the others. The rules ensure that your guests must talk to many different people – making this game an excellent ice-breaker.

UP JENKINS

Equipment: Coin

Preparation: None

This is an ideal after-dinner game – and is liable to get very silly. The table must be divided into two teams who face each other. The members of Team One then pass a small coin to each other, under the table. The object is to confuse Team Two as to who has the coin. At any point the leader of Team Two may call "Up Jenkins". At this point, all the members of Team One must put their closed fists above the table. The leader then calls "Down Jenkins" and all the Team One members must slap their palms face down on the table. Team Two has to guess who holds the coin. If they get it right, the teams swap roles.

INSANE DELUSIONS

Equipment: None

Preparation: Think of as many 'insane delusions' as you can for your guests. Example: thinking they've got a ferret down their trousers, or that they've seen aliens landing, or they're the Queen.

Send one of the guests out of the room and assign delusions to everyone else. Invite the outsider back into the room to play the role of a psychiatrist. They must discover everyone's delusions by asking questions and watching their behaviour.

This is another great ice-breaker which will rid guests of their inhibitions.

THE IDENTITY PARADE

Equipment: A large sheet with a small hole in it, pencils, paper

Preparation: None

Assemble half your guests behind a large sheet. Each of the hidden players takes it in turn to poke his or her nose through a hole in the sheet. The players on the other side write down which nose they think belongs to which person. This is not as easy as it sounds, particularly if your guests have only just met! The winner is the person that has the greatest number of correct guesses.

THE LIMERICK GAME

Equipment: Pens and paper

Preparation: None

Each player writes the first line of a limerick and passes it to the person on their left. The next players in turn all add a line to the limericks they have been passed until they are complete. The limericks are then read aloud – with hilarious results. Alternatively, the first person may write the first line, and pass it to their left. The second player then writes down a word that must be included somewhere in the rest of the limerick, which the third person must complete.

DICTIONARY/CALL MY BLUFF

Equipment Pens, strips of paper, dictionary

Preparation: None

Fans of television's *Call My Bluff* will love this game. Player One chooses an unusual word from the dictionary and writes its definition down on a strip of paper. They then read the word (but not the definition) aloud to the other players.

Each of the players then writes down a definition for the word – it can be imaginative, mundane, silly or serious.

Player One then collects and shuffles the strips of paper with the true definition and reads each one aloud. The other players then have to guess which is the correct definition. A point is awarded for each correct guess. A point is also given to each player whose definition is mistaken for the correct one by another player. The dictionary is passed to the player on the left, until everyone has had a go. The player with the highest points at the end of the round wins.

THE DRAWING GAME

Equipment: Pens and paper

Preparation: None

Guests are split into two teams, and each team then writes a list of places, people, events, quotations – for example, Prince Charles, the Millennium Dome, "to be or not to be" etc. Each player in turn is then given a word to draw for their team. The team that correctly guesses the greatest number of words wins.

The only rules are that the artist can only answer "yes" or "no" to questions and cannot use numbers or letters in their drawing. A game guaranteed to relax even the most reserved guest!

SPOONS

Equipment: Pack of cards, one spoon less than you have players

Preparation: Make a list of fun forfeits – for example, the loser must wash the dishes, sing a song or share an embarrassing secret!

As this is not a sedate card game, you may wish to remove all wine glasses from the table before you begin.

If you have ten players, make sure you have ten cards of each suit in your pack (e.g., Ace to ten of Hearts, Clubs, Spades and Diamonds). If you have six players you will need six cards of each suit in your pack, and so on.

Put the spoons in the middle of the table. Shuffle the deck and deal out all the cards. On the call of "Go!" everyone passes one card to the person on their left and takes one from the person on their right. The first person to collect four of a kind shouts "Spoons!" – this is the cue for everyone to grab a spoon from the middle. The loser is the person without a spoon – and they must do a forfeit.

CHEAT!

Equipment: One or more packs of cards

Preparation: None

The aim of cheat is to be the first to get rid of all your cards – by fair means or foul.

Deal all of one or more of your packs to your players. Judge for yourself how many packs you need – though your players really need at least ten cards each. It doesn't matter if some players have one more card than others.

The player to the dealer's left puts any number of cards face down in the middle of the table, saying what they have played (two fives for example). They may tell the truth – or lie. The next player must lay down a greater number of fives, or some sixes. Again, they can lie if they want – calling four fives but actually putting down three twos and a four.

Players can miss a turn if they wish.

At any point in the game the player who has just called may be accused of being a "cheat", by one of the other players. They must then reveal the cards they have just played. If they have cheated they must pick up the entire pack. But if they have not cheated, their accuser must pick up the pack.

LOOK RICH – WITHOUT SPENDING A FORTUNE

That's right – you really can look rich without having or spending a fortune. It's the little things that set the rich apart. Here they are:

1. Keep an all-year round suntan. Only working stiffs are pasty-faced – the really wealthy upper crust follow the sun at whim and maintain tans the whole year. A cosmetic tanning cream will bronze your face, and nobody will be the wiser.

2. Wear natural-fibre clothing, like cotton, wool and linen – and don't worry about the wrinkles. Rich people love them on their clothes.

3. Wear neutral colours. The rich love white, beige, black, cream and mauve.

4. Don't wear gaudy baubles. They are too tacky for wealthy people. All jewellery should have the appearance of quality – so stick with gold and silver fakes.

5. Stay away from hair gels and garish hair colour dyes – simple hairstyles are the hallmark of class.

6. Drop names. If you need to know which names are worth dropping, check out leading trade magazines and newspapers.

7. Drop places. Not Paris or Rome, but out-of-the-way spots only a well-travelled, rich person would know about.

8. Carry a book with you – but nothing juicy. The rich are into self-improvement, business and philosophy. Or carry a foreign newspaper – you're checking on the political situation because your family has property there.

9. Don't carry cash. Top cats never have any liquid funds – they charge everything or use credit cards.

10. Buy small items in prestigious shops – top stores like Harrods have stationery and cards that cost little more than other places. It'll make people think you shop there regularly.

11. **Talk about spas or new health treatments** like the garlic-oil and papaya-enzyme pills you've been advised to take.

12. **Speak softly** – rich and successful people don't need to raise their voices to get attention, because they're used to being listened to automatically.

13. **Be eccentric** – the richest people around can afford to be. Go sockless and wear boating shoes: everyone will think you own a boat too; a sure sign of wealth.

ENJOY A FABULOUS HOLIDAY – FREE OF CHARGE

PFC tip: the easiest way to arrange a free holiday is to swap your home for a comparable property. The exchange is free, apart from the minimal cost of finding someone who wants to trade with you. Place an advertisement in an international publication. That two-minute call could get you free accommodation in a luxury villa in the Caribbean, a charming apartment in Rome, or a rambling ranch house in Mexico! Alternatively contact a home-exchange organisation. These companies publish directories several times a year detailing those people who are interested in swapping homes, when they want to travel, where they wish to go, and so forth. Useful contact: Homelink International, (01344 842642).

THE FREE SERVICE TO FIND A LONG-LOST FRIEND OR RELATIVE

Contact your long-lost friends and relatives – get in touch with the DSS. Write down everything you can remember about the particular friend or relative; information such as full name, maiden name, date of birth, last-known address, National Insurance number, and spouse's details. Then send a letter with this information to DSS, Tyneview Park, Whitely Rd, Benton, Newcastle-Upon-Tyne NE98 1BA, and ask them to pass it on to that person. **Bottom line:**

they're not obliged to – but sometimes do.

CATCH A BIGGER FISH BY USING A WOMAN'S PUBIC HAIR AS BAIT

You'll be hooking beautiful four pounders all the time! How it works: fish communicate using chemicals and have highly sensitive receptors to smell – and research shows they're attracted to human female chemicals which are at their strongest in pubic hair. Note: human male chemicals repel fish – use a man's pubic hair and you'll never catch a fish again!

ENJOY GREAT SEX – WHATEVER YOUR AGE

Great news: a recent US study of 50- to 70-year-old men and women shows that the vast majority of those who had partners remained sexually active. However, there are age-related changes that need to be dealt with – it may take longer to become aroused, erections may not be as firm, and you may need more time before you're ready for sex again. But you can still have a terrific sex life! Here are the secrets of successful sex:

1. Keep making love. If men continue to have sex regularly, they boost their potency – those that go without sex for long enough face an increased risk of becoming impotent. And women who have frequent sex keep their vaginal tissues more elastic and have improved vaginal lubrication. Regular sex also reduces stress and helps you to sleep. One Swedish study shows that older people who are sexually active have more vitality, greater intellectual ability and a better memory than those who don't engage in sex. It's unwise to compare your sexual appetites and performances with those of other people; we're all different – and many people exaggerate. It's important to bear in mind that what is 'normal' for someone else may be too much or too little for you. It doesn't matter. **Bottom line:** whatever you're comfortable with is fine; as long as you're happy and feel good about it.

2. Ask your GP about any drugs that you're taking; some can interfere with your sex life. Many doctors feel uncomfortable discussing sexual matters with their patients and won't volunteer information about a drug's side effects on your sex drive. If you deal with the issue directly they may be able to lower the dosage that you're taking, or could substitute the drug for another medicine.

3. Ask your GP to refer you to a gynaecologist if you're suffering from vaginal dryness associated with the menopause. They may be able to prescribe a hormonal treatment that will help. Alternatively, speak to your pharmacist; there are various over-the-counter preparations available from your pharmacy. Consider hormone replacement therapy (HRT) if hot flushes and thinning vaginal tissues are affecting your libido. You may want to try taking oestrogen, which is usually combined with progestogen, another female hormone. Sensible: start with the lowest possible dosage – it will often be all that's needed. And ask about adding androgens to the oestrogen mix. Some doctors are discovering that adding the male hormone to the standard oestrogen replacement regimen can boost sexual desire, although it is not common practice yet.

4. Have your DHEA levels checked by a doctor operating on a private rather than an NHS basis. Dehydroepiandrosterone (DHEA) is a hormone in both men and women that declines with age – and can affect your sex drive. But this hormone can be prescribed privately or is available via the internet; taken, it can restore your DHEA and libido. Contact: Optimal Health Centre, 19 Milford House, 7 Queen Anne Street, W1G 9HN, (020 7436 7713). Similarly testosterone levels can drop as you get older, with comparable effects on your sex drive. Injections of testosterone can be very effective – often, only one shot is needed and sexual powers are restored straightaway. Or, Viagra improves staying power in 70% of men; again, this may be available on a private basis or purchased over the internet – although it should only be taken as the final option as it is for impotence rather than recreational use.

5. Cut the fat from your diet. A University of Utah study found that eating fat-laden foods may decrease the production of testosterone. Also eating fatty foods puts more fat on to your body – and US researchers have discovered that the more body fat a man has, the less testosterone is likely to be generated. Fat also clogs up arteries including the ones pumping blood into your penis, and this can lead to impotence. Try a pseudo-vegetarian diet. Some people find that a three-month 'pseudo-vegetarian' diet works wonders on their sex lives. This diet allows you to eat fresh fish and free-range chicken. As a minimum, eat organic meat if you don't want to give up meat altogether. Also add vitamin E to your diet. This vitamin is extremely important for sexual function – no one really knows why. The easiest way to accomplish this is to take vitamin E supplements.

6. Go easy on alcohol. Although alcohol may put you in the mood for love, your body is less likely to respond if you have too much of it in your system. Alcohol impairs sexual performance. And stop smoking. World-wide studies have shown that men who smoke heavily are far more likely to be impotent than those who have never smoked or who have given up. **Bottom line:** smoking is known to contribute to the hardening of the arteries and will lead eventually to impotence. It is vital to take some exercise. Being aerobically fit enhances your sexual performance. Strenuous exercise may increase testosterone levels in men and improve the blood flow to all parts of the body, including your genitals. Becoming physically fit improves your self-esteem and makes you feel more attractive to your partner. Learn to meditate or do relaxation exercises as well. Anything that reduces stress helps your sex life.

7. Remember romance. Don't underestimate the effectiveness of candles, mood music, and sexy underwear. Discover what works for you and your partner; and go for it! And: consider an aphrodisiac. There isn't a scientifically proven magic pill available yet, but various medicinal herbs are known to help you. Chinese, Japanese, and Indian Ayurvedic specialists recommend certain herbs – winter cherry, liquorice, molucca bean, Indian kudjer and Indian gooseberry. Also watch a romantic or erotic film.

8. Schedule a sex session. There is no sense in trying to make love after a long and stressful day. Try to have sex in the morning or afternoon; and when you're not mentally and/or physically exhausted. Or get away for a weekend free from distractions. The absence of interruptions is often the best aphrodisiac of all. Plan for privacy. Distractions are the equivalent of a cold shower. Some couples set their alarm for the early hours of the morning. Be creative – try something new, such as making love in another room, massage, or taking a shower or bath together.

HOW TO BE THE WORLD'S GREATEST GRANDPARENT

Being a gran or granddad isn't always easy. But if you follow our step-by-step guide, you'll soon become a number one grandparent:

1. Treat all grandchildren equally. Why: children have very strong feelings of fair play and what's right and wrong. Guidelines: make sure your grandchildren receive the same amounts of presents, attention and cuddles. And: take the same interest in all of their hobbies, exams and jobs. Essential: never compare – for example, do not comment if one grandchild obtains a higher grade in an exam or has a better job than the others. Also: avoid taking sides in family arguments.

2. Speak about the past with your grandchildren. Fact: these conversations will become part of their memories. As a grandparent, you can bring a sense of continuity to children, whatever their age. Tip: the past often fascinates young children, especially those things that they have only read about or seen on television. Examples: your schooldays, the clothes you wore, what your childhood home was like to grow up in.

3. Talk about the present too – you need to be a vital, active part of the family. Idea: keep abreast of the topics that interest your grandchildren and they like to talk about. Example: watch the daytime television programmes that fascinate your pre-school grandchildren. Important: do be aware of children's changing interests, and grow with them. Grandparents sometimes forget that something that interested achild at five may embarrass them at ten. Examples: Sooty, Thomas the

Tank Engine, Postman Pat.

4. Be ready to listen to your grandchildren – this isn't always as easy as it sounds. Typical: you may feel that your grandchild's problem is insignificant. Remember: it is not a minor problem to the child – otherwise they would not want to discuss it. Example: the death of a small pet such as a goldfish or a hamster. Better: listen to what they have to say, and talk them through it. Wise: talk about your own experiences of grief, and how you came to terms with it.

5. Keep a confidence – you should never divulge anything that a grandchild says to you in secret. Problem: you may feel you should tell the parents what you know. But: this will lead to a loss of trust between you and your grandchild. Suggestion: explain how you feel to your grandchild, and ask if you can speak about what is concerning you to their parents. Alternative: persuade your grandchild to speak to their parents themselves. **Bottom line:** maintain that trust.

6. Share experiences with your grandchildren. Example: a grandfather could try a teenage grandson's hair gel; and then discuss the differences between hair creams and gels. Tip: it is these little snippets of conversation that strengthen a relationship. Do: always comment in a sincere way. Don't laugh at a teenager's clothes, hairstyle, or the way that they look. Remember: the fashions when you were young, and your parents' reactions.

7. Open up the lines of communication. Difficulty: you may live some distance away from your grandchildren. Good: keep a conversation going with letters, tapes and photographs – you could even go on-line on the internet. Note: you may not always get a prompt reply (or any response at all) but you will be talking to them – and they will remember. And: keep in touch by remembering their birthdays, sending a small gift or money as an occasional treat, and writing a postcard for them when you are away on holiday. Result: your grandchildren will be relaxed in your company when you meet again.

UNDERSTANDING DREAMS – UNCOVER THE TRUTH ABOUT YOURSELF

By reading the messages of your unconscious mind, you'll find it easier to identify and deal with your hopes and fears – and can go on to become a happier and more fulfilled person. Here's what to do:

1. **Record your dreams.** Do this as soon as you wake up as you'll remember them most clearly – so have a pen and paper beside the bed. Before you go to sleep, start a new page in your dream notebook and put the next day's date on it – this lets your unconscious know your intentions in advance. Knowing that you are going to take its messages seriously, your unconscious will make greater efforts – and you will be more likely to remember what you dream.

2. **Don't interpret a single dream** as it will produce misleading results. For best results, record a body of information about your dreams; and analyse a wider range to produce more accurate assessments.

3. **Eliminate (parts of) dreams that are not of a symbolic nature.** For example, re-runs of that day's events. But, do ask yourself why your unconscious has replayed those events – you may wish to subject them to a more detailed investigation. Also ignore any event that seems to be a response to a physical stimulus. Thirst or the desire to urinate may typically impinge upon your dreams. Ignore those dreams that refer simply to you and your own desires; wish-fulfilment and anxiety dreams.

4. **Interpret the remaining dreams:** they represent messages from your unconscious mind. Parts of the mind specialise in visual understanding and communicate through pictures or symbols. Often, symbols work by analogy. For example, if a blind person appears in a dream, then your unconscious mind may be pointing out some blindness in yourself; some obvious truth that your conscious mind is choosing to ignore. Symbols might seem bizarre and nonsensical, but could still contain an important message. For example, during a conversation, you're transformed into a flying seagull – your unconscious might be suggesting that you should 'fly away' from such conversations in future. Alternatively, the message might be that something

you've learned in that conversation could give you a new freedom – as symbolised by the seagull in flight. **Bottom line:** the meaning of a symbol depends on its context.

5. Learn the tricks of translation. Certain techniques help you to uncover the meaning of dream objects, people and events. Free association: simply see what that object brings immediately to your mind and so forth. For instance, if you dreamt of a cat, the first word that 'cat' might bring to mind is 'dog'; and this might generate 'bone', and so on. It's essential to keep going until you come to a word that sparks an emotional response, whether positive or negative. Then go back and see whether this word and what it represents relates to the meaning of the object in your dream. Dream amplification: place the puzzling dream object at the centre of your thoughts. Mindful of the rich cultural symbolism at your disposal – and that of your unconscious mind – consider the various qualities of the object. If you dreamt of a cat, you might consider the softness of its fur, the watchfulness of its eyes, its aloofness and its patience. Believe that your unconscious has picked the best possible way of symbolising what it means to tell you – and the quality or association that you are looking for should eventually become clear.

FOOTBALL CRAZY? HOW YOU CAN MARRY IN YOUR FAVOURITE STADIUM

The 1994 Marriage Act enabled local authorities to license a wide range of premises to hold non-religious wedding ceremonies. And since then, more than 2,000 properties have been approved – including stately homes, caves, ships and even football grounds. You can choose your ideal venue by asking these key questions:

1.Where exactly will the ceremony be conducted? Don't assume automatically that it will take place in the most attractive area; it could be carried out in a side room.

2. Which days and times are available? Bear in mind that the venue's primary function usually takes precedence over wedding ceremonies – if you want to marry on your favourite football pitch, you may have to do it on a weekday.

3. Do members of the public have access to the venue? Don't think about getting married at a tourist attraction if you'd prefer a quiet, private ceremony. Weddings attract crowds.

4. Who will be in charge of arrangements on the big day? It is essential that you make sure you meet this person well in advance and be certain that you have confidence in their organisational abilities. See if you like them personally and want them to play a special part in your wedding day.

5. How many parking spaces are available? Many city venues are desperately short of parking space; larger weddings may be better suited to out-of-town and country venues.

6. Are any other events being staged at the venue at the same time? It's important to select a time when nothing else is taking place so you'll have the staff's full attention, and you won't have your ceremony disturbed.

7. Where can photographs/video recordings be taken? Many venues will restrict photographs to certain areas and may ban video recordings altogether.

8. Who is liable for any damage? Arrange insurance cover if you are liable – particularly if you're marrying in a stately home full of valuable antiques.

9. How many weddings have you staged to date? Always take up references – but not from those hand-picked couples recommended by the venue's staff. Or, even better, ask for a list; then select your own at random.

BODY LANGUAGE GIVEAWAYS – KNOW WHAT PEOPLE ARE REALLY THINKING

Only a small part of successful communication involves the words we speak – far more is conveyed by how we speak – the tone of our voice, intonation and pauses. And even more is expressed by our non-verbal communication, or 'body language'. Experts agree that this provides over 50% of the impact of our message. Words tend to convey information, whilst our body is more likely to express our attitudes and feelings. Most people are unaware that they are sending these signals; nor do they know how to read them. When you know what to look out for, you'll be able to interpret people's meanings accurately, and communicate more effectively; in job interviews, workplace discussions and during meetings and presentations. And you'll be able to spot those unconscious gestures that tell you whether someone's secretly attracted to you!

1. Posture: the way that people hold themselves can provide clues about their personality. A firm, upright posture with eyes looking straight ahead is associated with confidence and health. Whereas drooping shoulders and neck suggest dejection, shyness, illness and other negative traits.

2. Personal space: we all have a subconscious sense of our own personal space, which consists of four zones – 'intimate', 'personal', 'social' and 'public'. Our space is so important to us that we become uncomfortable if someone gets too close. But we also say that people are 'stand-offish' if they position themselves too far away. You can sometimes judge how a person feels about you from how close they place themselves in relation to you.

3. Pointing: the way a person feels can be indicated by how they point their body. People usually turn to face the person they feel most sympathetic to; and turn away from those they feel unsympathetic towards. Also people point towards things they want – for example, if someone turns away from you towards the door or another person, it probably indicates where they want to go. If someone is beside you and they turn slightly to face you, they're demonstrating interest. If they continue to face forwards, they are remaining neutral. Turning away means that they wish to be left alone.

4. Eyes: these are the most expressive part of a face. When people encounter something they like, their pupils dilate and become larger whereas when they feel negative about something, their pupils contract. **Bottom line:** even though the pupils are small, they can vary in size quite significantly, and this difference can be detected by observant people.

5. Arms and hands: someone who folds their arms is often making a protective gesture – it can mean that they feel threatened or are in a defensive or negative mood. If you are trying to persuade somebody to accept your viewpoint, folded arms suggest that the listener is sceptical. And if their hands are gripping their upper arms or their fists are clenched, this attitude is being reinforced. Partially folded arms also signal defensiveness. This is usually accompanied by other gestures such as fiddling with cuffs, a ring on a finger, a watch or a handbag. Someone who keeps their arms unfolded is signalling that they feel confident and unthreatened. If they are rubbing their hands together, this often signals positive expectations. And rubbing them together briskly suggests an open attitude to what is being said and anticipated. Rubbing more slowly can mean that the person expects to be the recipient of good news.

6. Handshakes: a strong, painful grip suggests the person wants to dominate you. A soft, limp handshake may mean they feel in a weaker position than you and can indicate apathy. When someone reinforces their handshake by gripping your arm with their free hand, they're trying to indicate sincerity. Some politicians use this technique on walkabouts and alienate those people who are familiar with this trick.

7. Legs: crossed legs convey the impression of negative feelings such as shyness, disagreement or even anger. So, watch out for other negative signals that might be present at the same time. When the upper ankle of one leg rests on the knee of the other leg, the person is betraying a competitive attitude. And if the upper leg is clamped in place with the hands, a very firm position is being taken by that person. They're not likely to change their mind.

8. Copying other people's body language: one of the best ways of recognising whether someone is for or against you is to see whether they mirror your body language. When someone shares feelings or attitudes, they will often adopt a similar body language. For example: when one person crosses their legs, the other will do so too, almost as a sign of agreement. When they disagree, the body signals start to differ as well. You can copy other people's body language to win their confidence, minimise negative signals and maximise positive ones, to appear more confident.

YOU CAN BE A SEXUAL MAGNET

Some men and women have the knack of attracting people to them at parties and other social occasions. They're simply applying the little-known secrets of sexual attraction. And if you learn and use these skills, you'll become equally successful from now on. These are those skills:

1. Find someone – maintain eye contact with them. Looking longer than usual into another person's eyes shows your interest and it can make that person feel special. Widen your eyes a little. US studies show that sexual interest is revealed by wider-opened eyes and this can be arousing to the other person. Men and women were asked to look at sets of photographs of other men and women – one person in each pair of photographs had had their eyes enlarged via retouching. And these people were almost always seen as being more attractive! Practise widening your eyes by looking in a mirror. This can help you convey the right image. Be careful not to gaze at someone for too long – an intent gaze is alluring only when it is welcomed by the other person.

2. Create sexual attraction – use open body signals. When you meet someone you find attractive, you'll sometimes feel tense and nervous and your body language will often reflect these feelings. Examples: arms folded, hands clasped, legs crossed together. These closed body signals are telling the other person that you don't want them near to you. To make someone feel really welcome, you need to send out open body signals. Stand facing them directly, and put your arms at your sides. Keep your shoulders back and lean forward slightly as this shows attentiveness to the other person. Or, sit resting your arms on the arms of the chair to indicate you're very receptive to the person in front of you. Keep your legs uncrossed. If you can sit in a chair that's lower than their one, that person will feel more comfortable with you.

3. Build that sexual attraction – emulate the other person's body language. Mirroring the other person's position and movements reinforces the sense of being well-matched. For example, if they're standing in a relaxed manner, adopt the same position. When the person shifts position, copy that movement as naturally as you can. Try to move closer as you do so as this adds to a sense of intimacy. Once you're tuned into their body movements, you can start slowly altering your own, so you become more open and receptive. The other person is then more likely to start copying you without knowing it! And this ongoing mirroring of each other can create a feeling of great intimacy.

4. Develop this first meeting – use touch as and when appropriate. Maintain eye contact as you continue talking as this shows your interest in them, and what they're saying. And smile or nod your head often to reassure them. When talking, use hand gestures to indicate an appreciation of the other person. For example, 'Experienced people know...', and gesture towards them as you say it.

Bottom line: take up opportunities to touch, if and when you feel these would be welcomed. Touch their hand when making a point, maintain contact a little longer than necessary when passing a drink, put your arm lightly around them as you walk through a crowd. These all help to turn this first meeting into a longer-lasting relationship.